COOKING WITH WINE
AND HIGH SPIRITS

Cooking With Wine and High Spirits

A LIGHTHEARTED APPROACH
TO THE ART OF GOURMET COOKING

by REBECCA CARUBA

CROWN PUBLISHERS, Inc., NEW YORK

© 1963, by Rebecca Caruba
Printed in the United States of America

To my three stalwart gourmets,
who have eaten every dish in
this book—and survived!
Robert Caruba, Sr.
Robert Caruba, Jr.
Alan Caruba

CONTENTS

Introduction
A Few Thoughts on Planning and Preparation   5

Wines and Spirits
The Fortified Wines—Sherry, Port, Madeira, Málaga, Marsala and Vermouth   15
White Table Wines   23
Red Table Wines   29
Rosés   33
Sparkling Wines   33
Cognac and Other Brandies   35
Liqueurs   38
Gin   41
Vodka   42
Rum   43
Beer   44
Scotch, Rye and Bourbon   45

Recipes
Appetizers and Hors d'Oeuvres   47
Soups   55
Brunch, Luncheon and Buffet Dishes   65
Entrées—Seafood   73

COOKING WITH WINE AND HIGH SPIRITS   viii

Entrées—Fowl 91
Entrées—Meat 105
Vegetables 121
Breads 127
Sauces 131
Miscellaneous 137
Cakes and Cookies 141
Desserts 159

Index 177

Foreword

One has only to read a few pages of COOKING WITH WINE AND HIGH SPIRITS to appreciate its completeness and importance. Rebecca Caruba has gathered her facts and recipes with professional artfulness and loving care and has turned out a volume that merits a place on all gourmet bookshelves.

Yet unlike some of today's cookbooks, which are more frill than anything else, COOKING WITH WINE AND HIGH SPIRITS is a true working tool—what I call a kitchen cookbook rather than a library cookbook.

—ALBERT STOCKLI
Chef Director, Restaurant Associates

". . . I often wonder what the Vintners buy
One half so precious as the stuff they sell."

—*from* THE RUBÁIYÁT OF OMAR KHAYYÁM

COOKING WITH WINE
AND HIGH SPIRITS

Introduction

Many books have been published on the subject of wines and spirits. Why still another? This book is dedicated not to the "wine snob" but to the person who likes good food. It should help you to put a host of good companions—wines and spirits—to work for you whenever the spirit moves you. If you have not yet tried cooking with wine and spirits I hope it will stimulate your desire to try something new—and rewardingly different.

Vino Felicitas!

One of the enduring simple pleasures to be savored in an unsettled world is a glass of wine to grace a leisurely meal. There are so many delightful wines in the world from which to choose that one could not even begin to taste them all. They can subtly transform familiar dishes, and with a carafe of wine at hand you can indeed dine in style at home.

It has been said that "a meal without wine is like a day without sun." Wine adds zest to a meal and makes the food "light on the stomach." A number of minerals for body growth are to be found in nature's own gift of the grape. But even if it did nothing more than soothe tired nerves after a high-pressure day, a bottle of wine would be, to many, well worth its modest cost. An inviting menu which includes a fruit of the vine insures that one comes to the dinner table with keen anticipation, ready to enjoy good company, good food and good wine.

If you can learn to prepare—and enjoy—just one perfect dinner from the various recipes in this collection, you will find yourself amply repaid for your experiment. This book introduces you to the wonderful world of wine and spirits— including fortified wines, vermouths, sparkling wines, red, white and rose table wines, cognacs, brandies, cordials, liqueurs and other spirits, including rum, gin, vodka, beer, whiskey, Scotch, bourbon, etc. It also offers a wide variety of kitchen-tested recipes using these wines and spirits, together with suggestions for suitable wines or other spirits to accompany these dishes. Every recipe has been streamlined without the loss of authenticity.

The familiar wail that "It takes so long to cook unusual foods, yet we love to eat them when we go out," will be answered in this book. No dish included takes more than an hour to prepare. In fact, most of these recipes take little longer to prepare than the time required to reheat a frozen dinner. Moreover, many of the processed and frozen foods make up a diet of monotony and provide little in the way of a challenge for good or could-be-good cooks. However, even if your time and kitchen space are limited you need not put up with such thawed, reheated fare, if you are willing to take the time to learn how many foods may be harmoniously combined with wine and spirits. When you do, see if you don't find a new zest in your dining. Becoming a good cook, with a repertoire of tasty dishes, need not entail endless hours as a galley slave. By streamlining your methods and learning to wield a corkscrew in the kitchen you can become a better cook and give your old stand-bys some competition. You'll soon learn how much wine or other spirit to add just as you learn from experience how to season to taste.

With so many fine foods now on the market all year long which were once available only briefly in season, you can plan endless menus featuring a variety of good things to eat. Many people have tasted abroad foods which they have wanted to try again at home. Few know just where to buy the unfamiliar ingredients or how to prepare them to achieve the same delicious flavor. If this book does nothing else but inspire you to combine food and wine or food and spirits harmoniously, you will begin to realize the wide choice of fine dishes from all over the world that can be prepared easily and enjoyed at home. Herbs and spices frequently called for in dishes of European origin may be obtained readily in most communities. Asiatic flavorings may prove more difficult to find, but it is well worth the effort to track them down when you are planning to serve an authentic Oriental dish.

INTRODUCTION

As you become more interested in variations in cooking you will be surprised to discover that the good cooks of each country have their own distinctive methods for preparing and seasoning the same meats, fish and fowl. Cooks in different sections of a country may produce a variation of a dish, even if it is called by the same name, by adding ingredients that are grown or produced locally. Many famous dishes are the specialty of a region and are traditionally made in the mode of a center of that region, for example, Tripe au Caen.

While more women than men don aprons to make up the solid phalanx of the world's day-by-day cooks, they too often regard it as a duty, which cannot help but dull their attitude toward innovations in the culinary art. Many men have gained impressive reputations as natural-born chefs among friends who, until they sampled succulent dishes prepared by these cooks with a flair for flavoring, had no idea of their hosts' hidden talents. Men are often the first to investigate the fine wines and foods of other parts of the world. The contemporary emphasis on entertaining out-of-doors has also encouraged many men to venture beyond char-broiled steaks into the realm of cooking with wine. Their wives often share their husbands' pride in their accomplishments and then find that dining at home has suddenly taken on sparkling new dimensions for them as well. Because I, too, know the glow that comes from creating something which is good to look at and good to taste, I have long wished to share my own portfolio of dishes I have enjoyed. I hope this book will enable many to share these dishes with me.

Even if you are quite unfamiliar with the good vintage years or first and second growths, you need not have all the knowledge that wine experts possess in order to follow the many delicious recipes which include wines or spirits among their ingredients. In time you will learn to select the wines which impart the best flavor. Keep a record of the kinds of wines you try, and if a dish turns out particularly well, be sure to note the label of the bottle you used, so that you can easily pick it out again from a shelf lined with various brands. Treat that wine and others that have been the stars in your culinary triumphs as old friends—partners in your blossoming career as a gourmet cook.

There are wines in just about every price range, to fit both the modest household budget and a more lavish way of living—wines that make your meals marvelous simply by their addition to a dish. Many dishes, without the subtle flavor the wine imparts, could not properly be called by the names by which they are known abroad. For instance, a *poulet en casserole* without wine would be just a chicken stew.

Many of those who like to cook with wine are of the opinion that no wine should be relegated to the category of "cooking wine." Rather, they feel, the better the wine, the better the dish. But there is a matter of degree. You need not use a *rare* wine for the pot when a *good* wine will do, but you may use a dry or sweet wine unless one or the other is specifically called for. When wine is heated, as it is in cooking, the alcohol completely evaporates and all that remains is the wonderful flavor imparted by the grape. But remember that if a wine sauce is cooked too long, it loses its flavor and therefore the heat should not be raised above a simmer.

Wines from Chile and from California, from Hungary, from France and Germany, to name only a few sources, help meet the ever-increasing demand for wines to suit one's mood and menu. Some American wines, while they should not be compared to the quality wines from abroad, still are able to hold their own as excellent table wines. A number of American producers call some of their fortified wines—sherries, ports, etc.—by trade names. These are pleasant, unassuming apéritif and dessert wines which should not be considered as the exact counterparts of the European sherries, ports, and so forth, which are the products of particular regions where grapes are tended with great care and processed in time-honored ways until the wines reach the desired color, character, and taste. The more you serve wine, the more you will learn about it.

More and more Americans are discovering how the serving of wines with their meals enhances the dishes they accompany and realizing that they need not be expensive. If you should come across a particularly enjoyable wine, why not keep a record of it and start a "wine diary," with names, dates and the character of the wines? The excitement of acquiring a selection pleasing to both palate and purse can be a never-ending adventure.

Wines range in character from the very dry to the very sweet and it is up to each host or hostess to decide which wines are most pleasing in taste and which of those should be served with a particular course. Along with each recipe in this book is a suggested wine accompaniment, but if you prefer to make your own choice, remember that the simplest plan to follow in selecting wine is "the lighter the entrée, the lighter the wine"—without all the fanfare, ritual and mystery that have all but submerged the simple, age-old art of serving wine with meals. There is no law which enjoins you from serving whatever wine you wish with hors d'oeuvres, fish, fowl, meat, cheese or dessert. However, you will find that certain wines are the complements of certain foods and furthermore that a wine should enhance, but not overpower, the dish with which it comes to the table. Your own developing taste should serve as the primary guide when selecting a particular wine or spirit to accompany a certain dish. You may want a mild apéritif or a rather rich wine to go with light refreshments such as cakes or cookies. You may want a substantial port for a frosty night or a sparkling, delicate wine on a spring evening. Another time you may prefer the fresh bouquet of a Swiss white wine or the brawn of a full-bodied Italian red wine. There are simple table wines for everyday use and finer wines to offer special guests. Quality wines are produced in many countries. Some stay in their own region as they are too delicate to travel, while others are regularly exported and suffer no ill effects.

A FEW THOUGHTS ON PLANNING AND PREPARATION
. . . . for Good Cooking with Wine

Good meals may end with brandy or a liqueur and a demitasse, but they start with sound kitchen planning. Good cooking with wine requires organization and dependable equipment to simplify behind-the-scenes activity, so that you are relaxed enough to enjoy the meal yourself. This is true whether you have all day long to prepare a meal or just an hour or so before your guests arrive. Why not approach the preparation of a meal with the happy expectation of having fun in doing so, as well as pleasing those who will partake of it? On this note, you will eliminate unnecessary steps, as well as outmoded procedures and equipment, and channel your energy to the preparation of gastronomic delights. By following these streamlined recipes, you can produce at home the same delicious dishes you like to order when dining out in famous restaurants.

Take time out to determine unnecessary steps which you can eliminate in the preparation of a meal. Are you often so tired by the time a meal is ready to be served that you wonder if it was worth all that effort? See if your talents can't be put to better use—with immediate and delicious results— by learning how to cook well with wine, rather than just trudging back and forth in the kitchen, duplicating many movements which could be consolidated or reorganized. After you cut down your working time, you will derive real pleasure from assembling your materials for a delicious meal and skillfully creating from them a masterpiece for all to enjoy.

In order to speed up the process of putting ingredients together you may find it helpful to have the cupboard shelves, sink and counter in your kitchen adjusted so that you can reach bowls, dishes and pans easily. Two inches may make a world of difference in comfort if a working area was formerly too high or too low for you. A special baking corner, with all your equipment and supplies stored nearby ready for use, will cut your preparation time in half.

You may feel inspired to prepare several dishes at one time so as to have a larger quantity or greater variety of breads or festive desserts ready for use. For example, having a supply of cookie sheets on hand will enable you to make enough at one time to fill several cookie jars. You may want to keep some partially prepared foods in your freezer, if you have one, ready for finishing touches at mealtime.

One way to conserve time and effort, which can be devoted to concocting these dishes, is to be selective about the equipment you acquire and use. Your mother and grandmother may still be using equipment which is now quite outmoded. Just because it was good for their way of cooking—and larger old-fashioned kitchens—does not mean that you must have it or continue to use it.

Countless labor-saving devices on the market are available to the cook who knows how to use them to slice minutes off preparation time. No two people work in the same way, so you will have to find out for yourself which appliances will give you the best results and how to compromise until space and budget permit the acquisition of these appliances. For example, if you can't fit a wall oven or double-oven range into your present kitchen, make the most of the one you have until you can improve your facilities, or perhaps obtain an auxiliary electric baker or roaster to augment your range. You will find plenty of oven space an invaluable aid, so that you can roast or broil and also bake at the same time, if you wish. If you have several heating units you will not have to wait for one dish to be finished in order to cook another which may require a lower or a higher temperature. There are many motor-driven grills and rotisseries on the market which can also be used outdoors, weather permitting.

Efficient kitchen aids, from major appliances to ten-cent-store gadgets, can help you produce better meals with less effort, if chosen with care. There is no need to add every new houseware item on the market, but if you will take the time to see various new appliances demonstrated you can determine which best serve your particular needs.

You may decide you need both a blender and a mixer. A blender will smoothly mix, purée and blend liquids or pulps which are to be added to solids. Recipes which call for beating ingredients for several minutes are much simplified by

COOKING WITH WINE AND HIGH SPIRITS 8

the use of electric mixers whose metal beaters do not tire as wrists do. Of course, some batters, such as pastry and yeast doughs, require other techniques. Some cooks like to work with pastry tubes for borders and fancy decorations. A well-equipped kitchen should include various pans and molds. A good all-purpose vessel is an earthenware dish with straight sides known as a soufflé dish. For small-size families 1-quart casseroles and 7- and 8-inch spring cake forms and pie plates are standard equipment. Pots in 1-, 2- and 3-quart sizes are useful, with a 5-quart pot for soups and quantity cooking.

Many durable broil-bake platters and other oven-to-table dishes can be used for both cooking and serving. These are often handsome and save endless time. Food can be quickly prepared before it is placed in such ovenware and, when cooked, can be put directly on the table.

The new non-sticking silicone fry pans and electric all-purpose appliances have changed many traditional cooking methods. Many cooks have found low round skillets or fry pans better for cooking frozen vegetables than old-style deep pots. Because there is less space between the cover and the bottom of the pan, the steam is held in better and the frozen block cooks more quickly with less liquid than in a deep pot. Although some cooks prefer to steam foods quickly in pressure-cookers, the recipes in this book are not adapted to this cooking process. More flavorful results may be obtained from slower cooking, which keeps foods tender and minimizes shrinking.

Before you add one knife or "magic" peeler to your cutlery drawer, do learn its proper use. Different shapes and edges are designed for definite purposes. You will not need a rackful of knives if you buy a few basic tools and treat them as reliable helpers by keeping them clean and sharp. These should certainly include a serrated bread knife, which comes in handy for cutting delicate cakes; a carving knife, kept honed and used only for carving; and a French knife, which should be used for paring and chopping vegetables. Vegetables may also be chopped fine in a blender, but care must be taken lest they be pulverized. Just a few of the many gadgets on the market which are proven time-savers are shrimp deveiners, garlic presses, cheese grinders and string-bean cutters. Add to your collection at your own pace. Helvetia Fondue is a marvelous party dish. A warm and delightful ambiance ensues when your guests are seated around the table, dipping their forks into a common dish, and this *intime* effect is heightened by the use of special fondue pans and fondue forks. A sukiyaki pan is an exciting addition to one's kitchen equipment and a spring form (a cake pan with a removable rim) will prove to be an invaluable aid in serving pastries that are too delicate to withstand much handling. Consider, too, investing in a brandy flamer for heating spirits and flambéing a dish. However, if one's budget limitations preclude the addition of all or any of these accessories, substitutions may be made—a chafing dish for a fondue pan, a chafing dish or electric frying pan for a sukiyaki pan, and so on.

Often, even with a super-efficient, gadget-studded kitchen, the best-intentioned cook can come to grief over the simple matter of the measurement of wet and dry ingredients. In a conscientious effort to be sure to have plenty of every item called for, one is prone to overmeasure. Then, when the results are not up to expectations, one will undermeasure the next time—and again meet disappointment. Posting a list of frequently used measurements on a cabinet or cupboard door may be helpful.

All measurements should be level, unless otherwise indicated. A problem often encountered is the exact measurement of flour. You will have less flour if you sift it first and then measure it than if you measure it first and then sift it. Give the measuring cup several slaps on the side to settle the flour. This does not mean that you may press it with a spoon; the slaps will do. If there is still too much flour in your cup, out it comes until you have the correct amount. Then sift it. These recipes are based on this "measure first, sift second" method.

Another pitfall for unwary cooks in the matter of measurements is the angle at which you hold a measuring cup or spoon. For the safest results, always bring the cup to eye level, which means placing the cup so that it is level with your eyes —straight out in front of your nose. A set of glass measuring cups in 1-, 2- and 4-cup sizes is a good investment, as is a set of measuring spoons in 1-tablespoon, 1-teaspoon, ½-teaspoon, ¼-teaspoon, and ⅛-teaspoon sizes.

Some handy kitchen measurements to remember are:

1 pinch = ⅛ teaspoon
60 drops = 1 teaspoon
3 teaspoons = 1 tablespoon
2 tablespoons = 1 liquid ounce
4 tablespoons = ¼ cup
8 tablespoons = ½ cup
16 tablespoons = 1 cup
2 cups = 1 pint
4 cups = 1 quart
16 ounces = 1 pound
4 tablespoons flour = 1 ounce flour
4 cups flour = 1 pound flour
2 cups granulated sugar = 1 pound sugar
5 large eggs = 1 cup eggs
8 to 10 egg whites = 1 cup egg whites
13 to 14 egg yolks = 1 cup egg yolks
2 tablespoons butter = 1 ounce butter
½ cup solid butter = ¼ pound butter
1 cup solid butter = ½ pound butter
2 cups solid butter = 1 pound butter
1 square baking chocolate = 1 ounce
1 package unflavored gelatin = 1 tablespoon
1 cup shelled walnuts = ¼ pound
1 cup shelled pecans = ⅓ pound
1 package dry yeast = 1 ounce
juice of 1 lemon = approximately 3 tablespoons
juice of 1 orange = 5-6 tablespoons
1 tablespoon cornstarch = ½ ounce
1 tablespoon potato starch = ½ ounce
1 #1 (8-oz.) can = 1 cup

1 #2 (20-oz.) can = 2½ cups
1 #2½ (28-oz.) can = 3½ cups
1 #3 (32-oz.) can = 4 cups

If yours is a knowledgeable butcher whose temperament and enthusiasm for good meat, well prepared, make him inclined to cut meat exactly according to directions, you're in luck. However, if this talented character does not exist for you, you will find that these few do-it-yourself hints will come in handy. First, about pounding: There are two reasons for this procedure—one, to tenderize meat by breaking down an over-abundance of connective tissues, and the other, to make thin slices even thinner as for Veal Scallopini. Meat should be pounded on both sides on a counter-top or wooden board with either the flat side of a cleaver, a wooden mallet or the edge of a heavy plate. (When a recipe calls for flour pounded into meat, sprinkle one side with flour and pound on that side only.) Machine-tenderizing in a butcher shop is an entirely different process and not suitable for these recipes.

About cutting veal in scallops: If your butcher is not familiar with this cut, you can describe it to him as very thin slices cut from the leg of veal (veal cutlet) or from the rump or shoulder (cheaper). You may figure on eight scallops (large and small) from a one-pound piece of veal, the leftover pieces being used for stew or ground up.

Marinating: There is a dual purpose here—to add a combination of delicate flavors and to tenderize, thereby decreasing the cooking time. Since most marinades contain acid, they should be used only in glass or glazed (pottery), enamel or stainless steel vessels; and the meat should be turned with wooden forks or spoons—never metal. Refrigerate foods if marinating for over an hour. I have included in this book only recipes that make use of the marinade (or in some cases, most of it) in the finished dish, since some of the nutritive value of the meat goes into the marinade during the process.

Flaming (or flambéing): This is simply the process of warming the required spirit, pouring it over the dish while the food is still hot, touching a lighted match or taper to the edge of the pan (or, preferably, tilting the pan toward the flame of the chafing dish) to set the spirit on fire, and then letting the flame die down. Its purpose is dual—to impart the flavor of the spirit to the dish and to burn off excess grease. Occasionally the dish is flamed at the table to produce a dramatic effect. In doing so, make sure that both the food to be flamed and the spirits are warm, in order to ensure a good blaze. To heighten the effect you may spoon blazing sauce over food as you shake the pan. Another method of flaming, when done in the kitchen, is to heat the liquor in a small pan (do not let it boil) and to tilt it toward the flame of the gas stove so that it ignites, or (if your stove is electric) to touch a match to the fumes that arise. The flaming spirit is then poured over the food. Turn out the lights at the right moment and *voila!* the final touch of drama.

Once her party date is set, the unflurried hostess must see to it that her silverware, stemware, dishes and trays are clean and polished. Sterling silver and flatware should be used regularly as it becomes more beautiful with use. Larger serving pieces such as platters can be stored in protective bags when not in service. Many modern earthenware and copper serving pieces are equally useful and one finds the beauty of today's designs and the excellence of craftmanship put such pieces in even the most sumptuous contemporary homes. Buffet and chafing dish meals and informal help-yourself serving have replaced to a great extent the traditional many-course formal dinner. The latter kind of entertaining is slowly passing, along with the one-time butler and upstairs maid. Many of the recipes included in this book are ideal for buffet entertaining, but can also be served at the dinner table without help. The hostess-without-a-maid will enjoy the meal as much as her guests do, if she has planned ahead well, so that when she greets them she is relaxed, charming and looking her best— confident that all is well in the kitchen. Company cooking should not take any more extra time than that required to prepare a larger than usual quantity of food. With careful planning, almost everything can be done in advance, except for lighting the candles on the table. The marketing for the meal can be done at the same time as your marketing for other meals of the week. All items needed should be in the house well in advance of the special dinner, so that as many preparations as possible can be spaced over the day or two before. Some desserts can be made even as much as a week ahead and mellowed or chilled for a few days. Thus more time is made available for a few minutes' relaxation just before your guests arrive.

Plan your meals for a special occasion or your everyday meals around an attractive entrée—meat, fish, or fowl—keeping in mind its color and character and the color and texture of the vegetables you plan to serve with it. In planning a meal around fish, for example, you should plan to have a substantial vegetable and a satisfying dessert.

Just as simplification in marketing and in kitchen procedures can make a hostess's role much easier, so that she can entertain more frequently and share unusual dishes with her family and friends, a similar simplification is needed in the area of accessories, from wineglasses to ashtrays. There is a wide array of cloths, mats, napkins, centerpieces, trays, tureens, casseroles, plates and cups as well as stemware and barware from which the modern hostess can choose for her personal kind of entertaining, but if storage and serving space are limited, she soon learns which pieces are most versatile and can be used for many occasions. There is no need to have all sorts of glasses for various wines, and an effort to simplify one's stock will usually result in limiting one's stemware to a straight-sided, 4-ounce, sherry or port glass for apéritifs, a 6- to 8-ounce goblet for table wines accompanying a meal, a tulip-shaped champagne goblet or a flute-shaped goblet for sparkling wines (either of which can also be used as a water glass) and 3-ounce cordial or liqueur glasses; with the addition of highball glasses, 3½-ounce cocktail glasses, tankards, punch cups, Old Fashioned glasses, 1-ounce pony glasses, 1½-ounce jiggers and brandy snifters as desired. The ultimate in simplification of one's collection of stemware might be the choice of a 6- to 8-ounce goblet, footed and bowled, which may be half-filled for cocktails or used for highballs, on-the-rocks drinks, wine, brandy, beer and even ice cream or sherbet. Such a glass is not suitable for champagne or for liqueurs, but otherwise is most versatile and a boon to the hostess whose storage space and budget are limited.

In times past the problem of sediment in wine was met by careful decanting and by pouring the wine into opaque goblets. Handsome colored examples of the glass-blowing art, highly developed in Venice and Bohemia, are now likely to repose on the shelves of curio cabinets, since the clear, bright wines on the market today are set off best in transparent stemware. The pleasure to be derived from admiring, in a graceful goblet, a claret, burgundy, white wine or bubbling champagne is bound to whet one's appetite even before the first sip of wine is tasted.

Wineglasses should never be filled to the rim. Chilled white wines may be served in a glass which comfortably holds six ounces of liquid, but the same amount of red wine is usually served in an 8-ounce glass so that the glass may be swirled and the wine given a chance to breathe. With little difficulty the hostess can usually find a simple, but well-designed, 8-ounce wineglass which will do for most occasions. But if special glasses are to be purchased for champagne, it is well to remember that the convex side of a tulip-shaped goblet is designed to hold the sparkle.

Since the opening of a champagne bottle is usually a prelude to a celebration of some sort, the reader who likes good food will want to leaf through these recipes to find a dish noble enough to accompany the wine beloved for toasts. Or, if you'd like to serve champagne and feel in the mood for giving a party, but will have to settle (this time, anyway) for a less expensive entrée, perhaps a glance through these recipes from far and near will suggest just the right dish to share with neighbors or friends whom you would like to entertain less formally. Remember this: Champagne is the one wine that can be used before, during and after a meal and that can accompany *any* dish. "When in doubt, use champagne" is a good maxim to follow. You may enjoy browsing through the recipes first, and then, after you have a dish bubbling away on the stove or in the oven, sitting down to read a bit more about the wide selection of wines and spirits around which you can plan many an inviting menu.

Since the primary purpose of this book is to introduce you to the pleasure of preparing these varied dishes, the following discussion of wines and spirits, their composition and processing, will necessarily be an abbreviated one. For readers who wish to pursue the subject more thoroughly there are many guides and directories with detailed descriptions and analyses of viniculture, oenology and related matters dealing with the various distillations and metamorphoses of the grapes, grains and botanicals which are blended into the wines, brandies, liqueurs, whiskeys, etc., which are drunk today. It is the thoughtful host or hostess who adds still another dimension of pleasure by skillfully blending these good companions of the world of wine and spirits into *spécialités de la maison*. May their tribe increase!

WINES AND SPIRITS
The Fortified Wines
Including Sherry, Port, Madeira, Málaga, Marsala and Vermouth

The wines listed above are often favorite choices for modern apéritifs, but they are so versatile that they can also be used in a variety of ways according to the menu planned by the hostess. Although often served chilled before a meal, some of these wines are equally good served at room temperature after a meal, or used to flavor various dishes, occasionally in combination with other wines, brandies or other spirits. Of course, many kinds of wine, including champagne, may be served, when chilled, as apéritifs. This discussion is, however, limited to the group of wines known as the fortified wines, to which brandy has been added to stop the fermentation and hold the wine for shelf storage. The Italian and French vermouths are fortified white wines blended with a variety of botanicals. The best known wines which have received a boost of brandy to enhance their character are the sherries of Spain and the ports of Portugal. Others are Madeira, Málaga, Marsala and muscat wines.

Today ports and sherries are used both as apéritifs and as dessert wines (chilled for the former, served at room temperature for the latter). In France ruby port is served as an apéritif. Such fortified wines do not lose their flavor even if kept on a shelf for months at a time. In earlier years they were found to keep remarkably well—with the "assist" provided by the fortification—on long sea voyages. The modern hostess often serves these wines as apéritifs in straight-sided sherry glasses or over cubes of ice in squat, on-the-rocks glasses, which have become increasingly popular for the cocktails today. For dessert wines a sherry glass or a port glass (popular in Spain and Portugal) are used.

Sherry

The special pride of Spain, sherry is a product of sun-ripened palomino grapes, with some Pedro Ximenes used for blending. There is a natural confusion as to the names which indicate different types of sherries, which range from the pale, dry *finos*; the *amontillados*, which are *finos* that have taken longer to mature and have developed a somewhat nutty taste, while retaining their dryness and delicacy; the *manzanillas*, light, dry, aromatic *finos* with a somewhat salty tang; the sweet and rather dark *olorosos*; the *amorosos*, which are lightly sweetened *olorosos*; the cream sherries which offer good bouquet and flavor in rich dessert wines; *vino de pasta* (wine of the meal), a golden sherry; and so forth.

True sherry, one of the most popular preprandial drinks, takes its name from the town of Jerez de la Frontera in southwestern Spain, where it is made. Until its first fermentation is over, sherry behaves like any other wine. But as soon as the new wine has "fallen bright," it receives a dose of brandy. It is then left out in the open air in barrels, which are not stoppered and which are only seven-eighths full in order to leave room for the *flor* (flower), a film of yeast that forms on top of certain wines during fermentation. If the *flor* develops the wine becomes a *fino*; if it does not develop, the sherry becomes an *oloroso*—or fragrant—sherry.

This curious sort of secondary fermentation takes place only under the hot sun of the Jerez region. At this point the wines from a single grape-pressing, maturing in various butts, range from light, pale and very dry to dark, heavy and sweet varieties. A series of coded signs is used on the heads of the butts to indicate the eventual character of each wine. Then the wine is stored in the *criadera* (or nursery), where its development can be closely supervised.

The system under which sherry is matured and aged to meet the strict standards of quality exporters is known as the *solera* system. By custom a number of butts of wine of an exceptionally fine vintage are laid down. A few years later an equal number of butts of the same quality and type are placed immediately on top of the first tier, and a few years later still another tier of new wine of the same type is placed above the second, and so on up to five or six tiers. The sherry shipper is then ready to draw wine from the *solera* for bottling. The amount of wine required is drawn off from the lowest, or oldest tier. The ullage in this tier is then made up from the tier immediately above and that in turn from the next tier and so on to the top rank, which contains the youngest wine. When all the wine is drawn off from the casks in the uppermost tier, new butts of fresh wine, taken from the *criadera* reserves, replace the empty casks. In this way a constant process of blending goes on year after year, and a definite standard of quality can be maintained for generations.

The addition of sherry to a dish adds a distinctive flavor that cannot be duplicated. Remember, though, that its flavor is pronounced—two tablespoons will suffice where a half a cup of other wine would be needed. Again, because of sherry's inimitable but potent flavor, do not use sherry when the recipe calls for "any white wine." When sherry is called for, use either sweet or dry, unless otherwise indicated. Following are recipes included in this book which use sherry as one of the principal ingredients:

Appetizers and Hors d'Oeuvres
    Caviar and Egg Mousse
    Chinese Egg Rolls
    Crabmeat and Bacon Balls
    Lobster Rumaki
    Party Pinwheels
    Shrimps in Sherry

Soups
    Cream of Cucumber Soup
    Cream of Watercress Soup
    Mushroom Soup
    Norwegian Lobster Bisque

Brunch, Luncheon and Buffet Dishes
    Beef and Vegetable Aspic
    Pâté de Foie Gras en Aspic
    Shrimp Aspic
    Tongue à la Duchess of Windsor

Entrées
  Seafood
    Baked Shrimp Casserole
    Filet of Sole Cordova
    Filet of Sole Maroca
    Lobster Cordon Bleu
    Lobster à la Newburg
    Mousseline de Crabe
    Oysters Royale
    Paella
    Shrimp Marinière
    Shrimps Tempura
  Fowl
    Canard Bigarade
    Chicken Divan
    Chicken with Olives
    Coq au Vin

Crème de Volaille
Poulet en Casserole
Meat
Braised Leg of Lamb Bordeaux
Côtelette de Veau
Sweetbreads d'Anjou
Veal Scallopini alla Romano
Vegetables
Cauliflower Loaf
Sauces
Bigarade Sauce
Sauce Dijon
Miscellaneous
Wild Rice
Desserts
Sherry Pie
Syllabub
Zabaglione
Zabaglione Sauce

Port

As long ago as the reign of Edward III a treaty was signed between Portugal and England whereby Portuguese fishermen were permitted to fish off the English coast. This event, which took place in 1353, may have marked the first importation of Portuguese wines into the British Isles. Or it may have been effected through a later event. In 1659 the first British consul was appointed to Oporto in Portugal and a few years later a British wine merchant sent his sons to Portugal to learn about the wine industry there. They found their way to Oporto, where at a monastery in the Douro region they tasted a remarkable wine. To keep the wine in good condition for their return journey, they added a little Portuguese brandy to fortify it for the long sea voyage to England. This, it has been claimed, is the true origin of port as it is known today.

COOKING WITH WINE AND HIGH SPIRITS

Port is made from grapes grown in the valley of the upper Douro, fortified at vintage time and shipped from Oporto, Portugal. The limits of the district of the Douro have been fixed by law and the amount of wine to be made in each year is also fixed beforehand by the Instituto do Vinho do Porto. When the grapes are pressed their sweet juice begins to ferment, but before fermentation has transformed the grape sugar into alcohol, some brandy which has been distilled from the same grape wine is added to prevent further fermentation.

Port-type wines are made in the United States, Australia, South Africa and Canada, but these cannot be compared to the Portuguese ports in character.

There are two sorts of port—vintage and blended. Vintage port is made from a limited quantity of only the very finest wine in an exceptionally fine year. It is allowed to remain in the cask for two years and then bottled in the country in which it is to be drunk, rather than being allowed to mature in the cask, as is the case with ruby and tawny ports. Experts do not agree as to the length of time that must elapse after bottling before vintage port can be drunk, but it is generally conceded that it must age in the bottle at least ten and preferably twenty years. After forty years it deteriorates.

Blended port is left in the cask for longer than two years, after which it is blended with similar wines and bottled. When ports are young, they are full of color—a dark purplish-red. After a certain time in the cask, they lose some of their color and become ruby-red, when they may be bottled as ruby port. After an even longer aging in wood, they lose their brightness and are known as tawny ports.

Crusted port is not allowed to age in the cask at all, but is bottled at once and matures in the bottle for ten to twenty years, where it forms a crust. White ports are made from white grapes and are not considered an important wine.

Port, served with fruit and cheese, is a delightful conclusion to a meal and should be served at room temperature; and tawny, ruby and white ports, when chilled, make excellent apéritifs. Many dishes are enhanced by the addition of port. These include:

Soup
    Norwegian Strawberry Soup
Brunch, etc.
    Duck Baroque
Entrée
    Glazed Chicken Breasts
Sauce
    Cumberland Sauce for Game
Side Dish
    Swedish Avocado
Desserts
    Bananas al Cordial
    Syllabub

Madeira, Málaga, Marsala

One of the longest-lasting of the fortified wines is Madeira, which is made from varieties of grapes grown on the island of Madeira in the Atlantic off the coast of Morocco. Since 1700 about 10 per cent of spirits has been added to the wine, made from the Bual, the Sercial and the Malvasia grapes. The full-flavored, full-bodied wine is casked and then stored for several months in hot chambers. This is called the *estufado* system of aging. Madeira owes its individuality to this process and to the idyllic climate and volcanic soil of the island from which it takes its name.

From Málaga, on the south coast of Spain, comes the dark Málaga, popular as a dessert wine with the Spanish. These wines, like sherry, are processed under the *solera* system.

Marsala wines from Marsala, Italy (once called Marsa-Ali when this was a Saracen port of Ali) range from dry to sweet and are rather dark in color. The dry variety is sold in England as Virgen. The name, Marsala, alone indicates a very sweet wine with a taste of burnt sugar. Marsala, like Málaga, is matured in the *solera* system.

Try the following recipes to learn the flavor that is imparted by these rich wines.

Appetizers
    Crabmeat and Bacon Balls
Brunch, etc.
    Pâté de Foie Gras en Aspic
Entrées
    Duckling Marengo
    Oysters Madeira
    Lobster à la Newburg
    Veal Scallopini alla Romano
Breads
    Christmas Panetone
Sauces
    Sauce Dijon
Miscellaneous
    Swedish Avocado
    Wild Rice
Desserts
    Syllabub
    Zabaglione
    Zabaglione Sauce

Vermouths

French vermouth, more bitter in flavor than the mellower Italian vermouth, is made largely in Marseilles, from white wines, which become very dry as they mature. In order to give vermouth a characteristic mildness the better producers of vermouth use a *mistelle* or *vin de liqueur* (a form of brandy) in place of sugar. Some forty or fifty different herbs, plants, roots, leaves, peels, seeds and flowers are used in the manufacture of a French vermouth. All the botanical ingredients are put into a large tank. The basic wine is then poured in and left for a month. When the wine has taken on the flavor of the plants, it is drawn off and new basic wine added in its place. This is done four times before the flavor of the plants is exhausted. This infusion is mixed with other basic wine and alcohol is added to raise the alcoholic content of the wine to 19 per cent. To properly prepare and mature a true French vermouth takes almost four years.

Italian vermouth, a sweeter apéritif, is also made from white wines that have been caressed with fragrant herbs. The characteristic sweetness stems from the fuller, naturally rather sweet, white muscatel grape that is used. It contains 15 or 16 per cent alcohol and rather more sugar than alcohol. In Italy vermouths must be made from wines that are at least one year old. The method of processing it is almost the same as that used for French vermouth.

Other light and gay appetizer wines include the French apéritif known as Pikina, which contains quinina and orange; the anisated PEC, which also contains certain other undisclosed ingredients; bitter-sweet Punt e Mes from Italy; Cynar, a vermouth with an artichoke essence; Chamberry Fraise, a strawberry-flavored vermouth; delicate Lillet; and many other mild aromatic wines.

Vermouth is excellent for basting roasts and adds its own special magic to dishes such as Steak Diane, Lobster Supreme, and Mousseline de Crabe.

White Table Wines

There are many delightful table wines of all kinds—white, golden, straw-colored, red, purplish, rose in color—impossible to list here and too many to taste in a lifetime. White wines are made from either black or white grapes by fermenting the juice after the skins are removed. The label on a bottle will tell you what kind of wine it contains and where it comes from. It may also offer a few suggestions as to which dishes go very well with it. Try a variety of wines when you dine out and at your own table and you will gradually learn the difference in taste, bouquet and color of various wines and the flavors they impart to the dishes you create.

The classic European white wines are fairly well known, but many modestly priced American white wines are also at hand. Nearly 90 per cent of American wines come from sunny California vineyards, such as the famed Napa Valley. The rest of the American wines come from the Finger Lakes region of upper New York State, in the vicinity of Lake Keuka and Lake Canandaigua, as well as from Ohio and a few other states. American wines sold under familiar European labels —Sauternes (called "Sauterne" in America), Chablis, Rhine wine—are often excellent, but should not be regarded as the equivalent of the European wines of the same names, which are produced under certain conditions in certain regions of Europe.

Europe offers a vast wine list—there are some 50,000 registered German wines—and France, which is the largest producer of wines (more than ten times the annual American output), has to import still more wine to satisfy all thirsts and special tastes.

Of the world's white wines, the Rhine wines of Germany from the terraced vineyards of the Rheingau, the Mittelrhein and the Rheinhesse that line the river have many devotees. Other famed vineyards are the Moselle valleys and lower Franconia, the Nahe valley and the Palatinate. The noble grape of the Rhine and Moselle vineyards is the Riesling, a small grape which, while it does not produce abundantly and ripens very late, is one which, when nature smiles, gives a glorious wine. The Oestreicher, Traminer and Sylvaner grapes are grown in the Rheingau, the Rheinhesse, the Rheinpfalz and lower Franconia.

The unique quality and distinguishing characteristic of German wines is their natural tartness which makes them clean on the palate. "Rhineland is wineland" is an old German proverb. From the Rhine and its tributaries come fine Moselle wines, noted for their clean, light freshness; the Rhine wines, among the world's finest for their balanced harmony, flavor and bouquet; the Palatinates, with their special fire, body and natural sweetness, as well as a number of other distinctive vintages.

Between Saarburg and Coblenz, along the banks of the Moselle, can still be seen the ruins of numerous Roman military posts. Cultivation of the grape in this area is at least as old as the Roman era. Terraces blanket the slopes as high as the land can be cultivated. Centers for really fine wines are Traben-Trarbach, Zeltingen, Bernkastel, Piesport and Brauneberg, from which wines of the region receive their names.

Between Bingen and Coblenz lies the area known as the Mittelrhein (Central Rhine), with vineyards on steep mountain slopes. The area along the northern bank of the bend in the Rhine is called the Rheingau. Opposite Rüdesheim, near Bingen, the Nahe flows into the Rhine. The wine produced near the mouth of the river is characteristic of the region and its clean, dry taste considered by some as the best of the German wines. South of Worms is a plateau extending to the Swiss border on which there are planted many vineyards. The wines are sweet because of the quality of the sun and soil here. Some lesser wines are produced in other sections of Germany for home consumption.

The label on a bottle of German wine should tell you the name of the town and the name of the vineyard and should inform you as to whether or not the wine was estate-bottled at the vineyard by the owner. If the wine is bottled in another section of the district, the label should also tell you that. Certain descriptive phrases on a label also supply valuable tips for the knowledgeable wine purchaser regarding the quality of the wine. A label marked *Spaetlese* means that the grapes were picked late and contain less juice and more sugar, thus producing a fuller, fruitier, sweeter wine. The label may read *Auslese*, which means a pure natural wine obtained from especially selected, individually picked, fully-ripened grapes. A label reading *Beerenauslese* indicates wine made from selected, overripe grapes from the best location in the vineyard. The label *Trockenbeerenauslese* indicates the topmost quality and a higher price, since the wine must have been made from a special strain of mold-touched, overripe grapes, which have shriveled away almost to raisins on the vine, then been picked individually and pressed separately. Of course, this type is produced only in very small quantities and takes some seeking out by the persistent wine-lover.

Alsatian wines are often called "French Rhine wines." Alsace lies on the west bank of the Rhine, which extends southward from Strasbourg to Switzerland, and it lies between the Rhine and the Vosges. This area has been an important wine-producing region since the days when the Roman conquerors occupied the valley of the Rhine. Alsatian wines are firm and "winy," yet at the same time fresh and flowery. They have a distinctive taste, yet are similar to German wines, since a great portion of Alsatian wines are made from Riesling and Traminer grapes.

The wines of France are as varied as they are excellent. Fine wines come from Burgundy, Mâcon, the Rhone Valley, the Loire Valley, Provence and Bordeaux. The choice of white French table wines is wide, and you will find that a happy epicurean experience ensues when white wine is added to certain Continental dishes and a glass of the same wine is served with that course. The white wines of Burgundy include Montrachet, Meursault and Chablis. Pouilly-Fuissé is one of the most popular choices today. The most famous name among the Sauternes is, of course, the noble Château Y'Quem, a heavy, sweet wine of the first growth. Light, dry, white wines, such as Graves, are made from grapes grown on particularly gravelly soil. Other notable names include Barsac, Corton-Charlemagne, Beaujolais Blanc, and Vouvray.

Swiss wines, known for their fine bouquet, are often enjoyed with cheese and fish. Most of them are of the dry, white variety, with each Swiss canton producing its own particular wine. The three principal wine-producing districts are Vaud, Valais and Neuchâtel. Geneva wines, from such villages as Peissy, Russin and Satigny, are dry and light, with a delightful bouquet, and should be drunk while young. On the west side of Lake Geneva are La Côte vineyards, from which come robust, unsophisticated wines. Along the north and south shores of Lake Geneva are Lavaux and Chablais. Here the vines grow tier above tier high on the mountainsides and must be cultivated with great care by hand, as the slopes are too steep for the use of machinery. Wines are believed to have been made in the area in the time of the Romans, but it was not until 1137 that the cultivation of the vine was spurred by the Bishop of Lausanne. Further east, near the end of the lake is Villeneuve. In the Rhone Valley are Yvorne and Aigle, which produce the best white wines of Switzerland, including Dézaley. Dry, flowery Neuchâtel wines come from grapes grown in a chalky soil, which makes them similar in quality to champagne. These wines have a life and sparkle ("the star") and should be drunk promptly after bottling and should be chilled so that their delicate freshness may be savored to the full. The city of Neuchâtel, in the northern part of the wine districts of French-speaking Switzerland, is surrounded by old vineyards. It is said that vines were grown there in the 10th century around an ancient abbey. Labels of Neuchâtel wines bear such names as Auvernier, Cormondreche, Saint-Blaise and Cressier—all wine-producing villages of the region.

In the southernmost part of the French-speaking region of Switzerland, bordering on Italy in the south and on France in the west, is Valais, called "the old country." At certain times of the year the people of Anniviers, who work in the lower valley, come down from their homes in the mountain villages to their daily labors in the vineyards. In late October, when the harvest is over, they carry barrels of Glacier wine from Sierre up to their villages, where the wine is left to mature for ten years or more in casks made of larchwood staves. Water is scarce here and the local wines reflect the character of the soil. Wine made from Fendant (the French Chasselas) grapes, cultivated in the Vaud Canton, has a strong bouquet and is usually served with a favorite Swiss dish, the famous Fondue Valaisienne. Fendant and Johannisberg are light wines and Malvoisie, Arvine Ermitage and Amigne more full-bodied. These bright, lively wines are at their best while young.

From south of the Alps come the Italian white wines, delicate to sturdy in range. A few are sweet, such as the wines of Asti, but most are dry to very dry in taste. From Tuscany come the white Chiantis, not as well-known as the familiar raffia-wrapped reds. The province of Venezia provides a delicious white wine with a subtle bouquet, Soave. Terlano, a choice white wine with a fresh and mellow taste, comes from the valleys of Trentino-Aldo Adige. From Lombardy come Grumello and Valtellin, the latter a pale golden wine with a fine bouquet and great finesse. Frecciarossa, in both red and white varieties, is a good wine made from grapes grown on the hills of Casteggio.

Hungary, a leading wine-producing country of Europe, is primarily renowned for its fine Tokay. It produces many red and white table wines, ranging from very dry to very sweet. Among them are Rizling-Azemelt, a light dry wine with Riesling characteristics; Somlai Furmint, a fragrant, dry wine; Badacsony Rizling, a pale dry, full-bodied wine; and Szilvanyi Zold, a bit sweeter than dry. Hungarian wines, which, like Alsatian wines, are exported in long, slender bottles, are better for drinking than for use in cooking, although Hungarians do use their own wines in some dishes.

Chile, South Africa and various other countries also offer refreshing white wines for the dinner table.

The following dishes are made with white wines other than the fortified whites:

Appetizer
    Helvetia Fondue
Soups
    Bouillabaise à la Caen
    French Onion Soup
    Gazpacho
    Italian Holiday Soup
Entrées
  Seafood
    Filet of Sole Dugleré
    Filet of Sole Joinville
    Filet of Sole Marguery
    Filet of Sole Maroca
    Filet of Sole Walewska

    Lobster Flambé
    Shrimps Marinière
Fowl
    Capon au Champagne
    Chicken with Almonds
    Chicken with Olives
    Coq au Vin
    Duckling Marengo
    Duck Provençale
    Poulet en Casserole
Meat
    Austrian Pot Roast
    Benlose Fugle
    California Pepper Steak
    Côtelette de Veau
    Lamb Steaks à la Mode
    Ossobuco Piemontese
    Rolled Veal with Truffles

Salad
    Jellied Cucumber Salad

Sauce
    Béarnaise Sauce

Desserts
    Asti Spumante Mousse with Strawberries

RED TABLE WINES

Almost every wine-producing country offers a range of red wines, from rather ordinary reds, which are virtually a staple commodity and inexpensive enough to be used on the table every day, to wines of superlative quality which help to enhance special occasions and which are the products of the careful processing that insures a high standard.

France, of course, lays claim to top honors in its production of a variety of fine red wines, from delicate to regal. It has specialized in this industry since Richelieu stimulated viniculture in the sixteenth century. If one wished to know the French vineyards, one could tour the country through the

Champagne section, down to Burgundy, then on to the Rhone Valley, to Provence, up to the Loire and on to Bordeaux, the greatest of the wine-producing regions. Each section produces distinctive types of wine, since the soil and amount of sun and water vary from region to region.

Burgundy wines date back to the time of Caesar's conquest of Gaul. Roman legions planted vines from Italy, but when the wine of the conquered region began to compete with that of the mother country, the Emperor Domitian in 96 A.D. ordered the vines uprooted and the fields planted with corn. Fortunately, this edict was only half-heartedly enforced and today 60,000 gallons of the great reds alone are made each year.

Bordeaux wines vary from light and elegant ones to full-bodied reds, from those known simply as *rouge* (red) or *blanc* (white) to the noblest of the Château vintages. The Bordeaux district produces a remarkable variety of wines—there are more than 7,000 classifications. The *Premiers Crus* (First Growths) include Château Lafite, Château Latour, Château Margaux and Château Haut-Brion. Château Mouton-Rothschild, a Second Growth, should, in the opinion of many, be included in the First Growths also. Some of the sections of the Gironde district have local names which may be seen on labels—Margaux, Pauillac, Saint-Estèphe, etc. Wines of the Côtes are made from grapes grown on the hills between Garonne and the Dordogne, the best in the Saint-Émilion district. From Burgundy come the Côte de Nuits wines called *Grand Premiers Crus*, an indication of a particular growth or vineyard of exceptional quality. From Côte de Beaune come full-bodied wines of high standard. Beaujolais wines come from the Lyonnaise district. Some of the finest are from the Thorins vineyards and the Moulin-à-Vent section. The Côtes du Rhône wines include both red and white such as Vouvray, Hermitage and Anjou. The red wines of the Côtes du Rhône, which are full-bodied, are often mistaken for Burgundy wines. Not much red wine has been produced in the Loire Valley in recent years, as it is primarily a white-wine country.

As for the wines of Italy, the early Romans were good wine-makers and enjoyed goblets of snow-cooled wines at banquets. After the fall of the Roman Empire, the Church supervised the cultivation of many Italian vineyards up to the fifteenth century. Grape vines flourish so luxuriantly in Italy, and so many localities press their grapes quickly with little finesse, that most of its wines are cheap, but not rated as fine. However, some of its wines have since gained recognition. Its grapes include Barbera, Bracchetto, Grignolino, Nebbiolo, Pino-Nero and Sangiovese, and wines made from them take on the varietal names. (The California wine known as Barbera is, by the way, not often made from the Barbera grape alone. Another California wine with a similar name, known as Barberone, is not found in Italy.) Still other wines are named for a particular region or given a special name by their producers. Wines from the Piedmont in northern Italy include Barolo, a purplish wine with a fine aroma; Barbaresco and Freisa, red wines of repute; Grignolino and Nebbiolo. Lagarino Rosato, a pleasing and delicate ruby-red wine, comes from the valleys of Trentino-Alto Adige. Bardolino comes from the vineyards on the shores of Lake Garda near Verona. A light, pleasing wine of a deep ruby color and with a delicate bouquet, Valpolicella improves with age. The Emilia section produces Lambrusco, a hardy wine. Corsica produces some robust red wines, whites and rosés, including Patrimonio, Cervione and Calvi.

The finest red wine of Switzerland, known as Dôle or Dôle de Sion, has a unique gun-flint taste because of the soil in which it is grown. Some of Hungary's best red wines, labeled Borosbor, are Kadarka, Szekzard, Egri Bikaver and Villany-Pecs. Spain exports a good inexpensive wine called Clarete from the Rioja district. One may find there red and white wines of a sound quality with an aromatic bouquet. Wine is produced also in Valdepeñas and Estremadura produces a red wine. Vineyards in many other countries in the world, including some in South America, South Africa and Australia, also produce good inexpensive red wines which grace dinner tables around the world. Spaghetti and chianti need not be your only duet. Why not see that your family's next pot roast comes to the table well-permeated with a sturdy red wine? Or make next Sunday's chicken a *coq au vin?*

Some American producers have adopted the custom of naming their wines after the varietal name of the chief grape used, so that the purchaser of a bottle labeled Niagara, Delaware or Elvira, for example, may expect a consistent quality each time. If a "Pinot Noir" is specified, instead of just a "red wine" or a "burgundy," the purchaser can rely on the fact that the wine is made from the true grape type, as stated on the label. California produces a number of varietal wines such as Cabernet Sauvignon, which is somewhat similar to a red Bordeaux; Pinot Noir, which is a Burgundy-type; Gamay-Beaujolais, which is similar to the French Beaujolais; Barbera and Grignolina, similar to the Italian wines of the same name. Of course they cannot be expected to match the European wines exactly, since soil, sun and water all subtly alter the character and taste of the grape. The red wines produced in the East are quite different in taste from the California red wines, let alone European red wines. Their labels sometimes read "New York State Burgundy" or "Claret" or just "Burgundy." Such wines should be regarded primarily as light-bodied, pleasant wines, which are good but not extraordinary companions.

When a recipe calls for "red wine" or "white wine," please understand that a *table* wine is indicated, not a fortified wine. Here are some red wine recipes—Continental as a sidewalk café.

Soups
    Minestra di Pasta e Fagioli
    Minestrone, Tuscan Style
Entrées
    Baked Western Steak
    Barbecued Potted Beef
    Boeuf à la Bourguignonne
    Braciola

Braised Beef with Red Wine
Canard Bigarade
Chili con Carne y Frijoles
Coq au Vin
Cornish Hen Plymouth

Vegetables
Baked Vegetables Brazilian
Burgundy Onions
Onions Aleatico
Red Cabbage with Wine

Sauces
Barbecue Sauce
Bordelaise Sauce
Spaghetti Sauce alla Piemontese

Rosés

Many modern hostesses like to keep bottles of pink wines on hand, as well as white and red wines, since they are pleasant accompaniments for not too hearty dishes such as fish, light meat and fowl, creamed dishes, casseroles, etc. They are usually served chilled in attractive stemmed glasses and lend a charming and delicate touch to many party menus. The rosy shade of the wine is the reason for the French name, *rosé*. The Tavel rosés, made in California from the same grape, are highly regarded. In the processing of the shimmering pink wines the dark grapes are pressed but lightly and the pulpy mass separated from the juice quickly, so that the basic color is kept light and the flavor delicate. The rosés do not keep well for more than a few years. The flavor is not pronounced enough to make the rosés suitable for use in the preparation of food.

Sparkling Wines

Sparkling wines are produced in France, Italy, Germany, Portugal and many other countries. Their bubbles seem to stimulate light-heartedness. Noted wine expert, Andre L.

Simon, divided them into two types. "The best," he said, "are wines the fermentation of which is completed after they have been bottled and securely corked, so that the carbonic acid gas, a by-product of fermentation, cannot escape and remains in solution in the wine; the prototype of these sparkling wines is sparkling champagne. The others are still wines which are rendered effervescent by having some carbonic acid gas forced into them at the time of bottling; the said carbonic acid gas may have been generated by their own fermentation in a closed tank, saved and used again, or it may be any carbonic acid gas; it makes no difference. Most sparkling wines are white wines, which are better than red sparkling wines, which, however, have their admirers." Some parties seem gayer with a bottle of sparkling Burgundy on the table. There are also some sparkling rosés, which are pleasing to many.

Although not as well known as champagne, other sparkling wines are made with the same skill, care, patience and experience. Lacrima Christi, dry and with an excellent aroma, is associated with Campania in Italy. Another famous sparkling wine is Asti Spumante. The term "Champagne" actually refers only to a wine from a certain district of France which is made from only four kinds of grapes, the black Pinot, Petit Meslier and Arbaine and the white Chardonnay.

It is to the monk, Dom Pérignon, cellarmaster of the Benedictine Abbey of Hautvillers, that we owe the credit for evolving in the mid-seventeenth century the first batch of champagne from still wine. He noticed that once in a while a bottle would develop bubbles or sparkles by a natural force and decided to investigate this intriguing phenomenon. It seemed that the wine actually went through a second fermentation stage in the spring. Through years of experimenting he was able to control this second fermentation. Dom Pérignon is also credited with initiating the use of corks in champagne bottles. He noticed the cork stopper on a bottle of wine carried by a Spanish monk who visited the abbey. Up to this time rags or wax had been commonly used to retain the liquid in a wine bottle. The monk promised to send some of the rough corks from Spain to the Abbey of Hautvillers and so, from the chance meeting of two monks, came the first of a long line of champagne corks . . . and a myriad of toasts.

Whenever a bottle of champagne is opened it should be consumed, since it is impractical to recork it. For this reason champagne is bottled in a wide range of sizes:

A split (or nip) contains 6½ ounces (2 glasses)
A half-bottle contains 13 ounces (4 glasses)
A bottle (or quart) contains 26 ounces (8 glasses)
A magnum (2 quarts) contains 52 ounces (17 glasses)
A jeroboam (or double magnum) contains 104 ounces (34 glasses)
A rehoboam (6 quarts) contains 156 ounces (52 glasses)
A methuselah (8 quarts) contains 208 ounces (69 glasses)
A salmanazar (12 quarts) contains 312 ounces (104 glasses)
A balthazar (16 quarts) contains 416 ounces (138 glasses)
A nebuchadnezzar (20 quarts) contains 520 ounces (179 glasses)

Leftover sparkling wine which has become still can be put to good use in a special dessert, for example Asti Spumante Mousse with Strawberries. Other recipes using sparkling wines are Capon au Champagne and Peach Bowl.

COGNAC AND OTHER BRANDIES

For many connoisseurs of good food nothing can take the place of a glass of cognac or brandy after a fine dinner and nothing can compare with these volatile spirits when it comes to flaming fruits and liqueurs or a holiday plum pudding.

Brandy is made by distilling the fermented juice of grapes or of fruits such as cherries, apricots or apples; and Cognac is the shining star of the brandies, once described as the "liquid gold which sleeps in casks and seems to be made of the distilled rays of the sunrise." A true Cognac is made by a very special process from grapes grown in the delimited region of Charente, where the little town of Cognac is found. The grapes are pressed but lightly and allowed to ferment by natural means. The resultant wine is then distilled by the pot-still method (rather than the patent-still) in almost precisely the same way as it was in the eighteenth century. In this method the wine is distilled and re-distilled by a highly complicated process so that the subtle flavor and aroma of the brandy is maintained, while all the undesirable elements are cast off.

In the Middle Ages taxes were levied on any undistilled wines exported from Cognac and the vintners decided to distill their wine in order to avoid paying such taxes, planning to restore it to its original state on arrival at its destination. When the importer tasted the distilled product, it was decided to leave it just as it was. It was called "Brandvin" (burnt wine) because it was distilled, and through the years became better known as "brandy." Although brandies are primarily French spirits, they are produced in many parts of the world as well as in France—for example, Spain, South Africa, Australia, Greece, Switzerland and California. They are always matured in a cask—never after they have been bottled—and, in the case of true Cognac, in casks made from a particular type of hard oak that is found in the Forest of Limousin, since this wood joins the grape in imparting the special flavor that is Cognac's. The label on the bottle indicates the length of time the distiller has aged his brandy in the cask before bottling it.

Fruit brandies are made by distilling the wine of fruits such as apples, plums, cherries and apricots. A very special kind of brandy is kirsch, which is distilled from the fermented juice of pears, raspberries, blackberries or cherries. In Alsace some of the cherry stones are crushed with the fruit, imparting a faint almond-like flavor to the brandy.

Recipes which include Cognac, kirsch or other brandies follow.

Appetizer
    Helvetia Fondue
Brunch, etc.
    Baked German Pancakes
    Pâté de Foie Gras en Aspic
Entrées
    Boeuf à la Bourguignonne
    Braciola
    Braised Beef with Red Wine
    Braised Leg of Lamb Bordeaux
    Canard Maison
    Chicken Cacciatora Piemontese
    Coq au Vin
    Duck Provençale
    Lobster Flambé
    Lobster à la Newburg
    Lobster in Shells
    Paupiettes de Veau aux Truffes
    Saltimbocca
    Steak Diane
    Sweetbreads d'Anjou
Sauce
    Sauce Dijon
Cakes and Cookies
    Swedish Apple Cake
Desserts
    Apricot Cream Mold
    Bananas al Cordial
    Banana Soufflé Flambé
    Cherry Sauce
    Chocolate Rum Mousse
    Eggnog Chiffon Pie
    Fig Soufflé
    Grand Marnier Mousse
    Grand Marnier Soufflé

Hot Chocolate Soufflé
Orange Mousse
Peach Bowl
Pineapple Soufflé
Strawberry Cream

Liqueurs

Jewel-colored liqueurs (or cordials) lend themselves to the flaming of festive desserts because of their high alcoholic content. They may be served as after-dinner drinks in clear 1-oz. pony glasses, poured over ice cream in parfaits or over sherbets or used in a variety of attractive fruit desserts.

Liqueurs are prepared by combining a neutral spirit or brandy with a flavoring or blend of flavorings and adding sugar syrup. There are almost as many kinds of liqueurs as there are flavoring agents. Almonds, anise, caraway seeds, cacao, coffee and vanilla beans contribute flavor, as well as cinnamon, orange peel, ginger and mint. Flowers, seeds, herbs and spices are compounded to make liqueurs—apricot, blackberry, black currant, cherry, grapefruit, orange, peach, pomegranate, rose, sloeberry, tangerine and violet.

Fruit-flavored liqueurs are usually made by the infusion method. For example, fresh peaches and dried peaches are placed in a cask containing brandy or neutral spirits. The fruit is allowed to steep in the brandy from six to seven months, during which time the brandy absorbs the color, bouquet, aroma and taste of the fruit. At the end of that time the brandy is drawn off and strained, sugar syrup is added and the mixture is aged for a year or so in a vat or crock in which the same type of liqueur has been stored previously. It is then filtered and bottled.

Liqueurs made from plant seeds, roots or herbs are usually produced by distillation. The principal flavoring ingredient is macerated in brandy for 3 or 4 days and the mixture is placed in a pot still. Simple syrup is added to the liqueur, which is aged in a vat for a certain length of time. Many of the vats are used from generation to generation.

Some cordials and liqueurs have a base other than brandy. Bacardi elixir is made from rum, sloeberry liqueur from sloe gin, drambuie from Scotch whiskey, Irish mist from Irish whiskey and rye cordial also from rye. Some liqueurs, such as Chartreuse, are prepared from a secret formula, the private property of members of the same religious order, which has distilled it for centuries. The monks secretly prepare the herbs and spices in an upper room and the botanical mixture is funneled into the vats of a distillery on a lower floor, so that there is no opportunity for observers to learn the formula.

Serving brandy or liqueur and coffee after dinner at the table, or after your guests have left the table and are seated in the living room or library, adds a touch of elegance to the meal and provides a relaxed and gracious finish. Coffee served in demitasses and tiny glasses of liqueurs are in a sense the perfect complement to a well-planned and well-prepared dinner and even today's busy hostess finds it a ceremony that is not a chore. If hers is a well-stocked bar, several choices of liqueurs may be offered, but one alone will suffice. A charming little ceremony ensues when the hostess places a cube of sugar in a flaming spoon or a demitasse spoon, flames it with brandy and passes one to each guest to be stirred into his coffee.

The transition of liqueurs from dining or living room to kitchen is an easy one as will be seen from the recipes that follow. The secret is to match the cordial to the main ingredient—for example, fish with orange liqueur, pork with ginger brandy, ham with cherry brandy, chicken with peach brandy, fruit desserts with a cordial that complements or with a matching fruit liqueur. You will want to try the delectable desserts incorporating liqueurs that I have chosen for this book, but on those occasions when an exotic dessert or first course is needed for the meal and lack of sufficient time precludes your making a soufflé, a mousse, a pudding or whatever, consider a simple fruit-and-cordial combination. Your own good taste will guide you in choosing a liqueur for a particular fruit, but as a starter you might like to think in terms of the following combinations of fresh fruits and liqueurs. (Frozen or canned fruits can be used, but they will not produce the same effect.)

Apricots with brandy or kirsch or Cointreau

Peaches with kirsch or Grand Marnier

Citrus fruits with Cointreau, Benedictine, B & B, or crème de menthe

Bananas with brandy (blackberry, apricot or cherry) or Chartreuse

Pineapple with kirsch, Cointreau, Triple-Sec or crème de menthe

Berries with kirsch, cherry cordials, crème de cassis, or Cointreau

Pears with kirsch, crème de menthe or crème de cacao

Or consider a macedoine of fruits (all kinds of fruits in season, cut up, flavored with liqueur, and chilled).

To combine fruits and liqueurs add to them first fine sugar or canned fruit syrup or simple syrup. To make the latter, boil 1 cup of water, 1 cup of sugar and ⅛ tsp. salt together for 15 minutes and flavor, if desired, with cooked, julienne orange or lemon peel (colored parts only). Then add liqueur or brandy and mix well. Chill thoroughly. If frozen or canned fruit is used, extra sugar or syrup is unnecessary. If fresh berries are used, sprinkle them with sugar, let them steep for two or three hours and they will make their own syrup.

Be daring and sparing. Daring enough to try new combinations of fruits and spirits (see chapters on wines, rum, etc.) and sparing in your use of the spirit itself. For fruits and cordials as described above, flavor each serving with one tablespoon of liqueur, taste, and add a little more only if necessary, remembering always that the aroma of the spirit should be suggested rather than pronounced.

Following are recipes that include liqueurs:

Brunch, etc.
    Chartreuse Pancakes
Vegetables
    Sweet Potato Puffs

Glazed Carrots Supreme
Sauces
Bigarade Sauce
Miscellaneous
Honey-Orange Dressing
Hawaiian Salad Dressing
Cakes and Cookies
Apricot Bars
Coffee Bavarian Cream Cake
Fudge Rounds
Orange Marmalade Cake
Pineapple Chartreuse Pâtisserie
Sicilian Cheese Cake
Sponge Roll
French Apricot Cream Filling
Zuppa Inglese Cake
Desserts
Bananas Chartreuse
Banana Soufflé
Bread Pudding Supreme
Chocolate-Orange Mousse
Mocha Mousse
Orange Mousse
Queen's Pudding
Strawberries Romanoff
Grand Marnier Soufflé

Gin

Gin is produced from alcohol which has been diluted with water and flavored (preferably during the distillation) with juniper berries, cassia, cinnamon, cardamon, coriander, lemon or rose petals, in combinations that vary according to the distiller. Gin, like vodka, is usually colorless, but there are gins that have taken on a golden hue as a result of their being allowed to mellow in oaken casks for two years or more.

The three principal gin-making countries, the United States, Holland and Britain, usually employ grain (maize,

COOKING WITH WINE AND HIGH SPIRITS 42

malted rye or unmalted rye) in making the alcohol for gin. Although occasionally aged in wood, gin does not keep well in the bottle and if kept too long, will flatten in taste or acquire a somewhat bitter flavor.

The before-dinner Martini is, in this country, possibly the most popular way of serving gin at this hour, although it can be served neat as in Holland (where it is called Schnapps) or as the main ingredient in a myriad of cocktails. Gin-and-tonic, as a long, cool drink, has gained enormously in popularity in America in the last few years, taking first place away from the once ubiquitous Tom Collins.

Turning from the bar to the kitchen, one finds that gin imparts a subtle flavor all of its own to dishes that might seem quite ordinary without the spirit. Cornish Hen Plymouth and Chicken and Gin on the Spit (see pages 98 and 96) are excellent examples of the magic performed by the addition of gin to the other ingredients, and having tried them, the imaginative cook is inspired to go on to new and greater achievements in the culinary use of this delicate flavoring.

Vodka

Long a Russian favorite, this clear liquor without the distinctive perfume of gin and with a deceptive potency in its high-proof depths has become increasingly popular in this country in recent years. It is made from a rye-malt or potato starch and is rectified and filtered to the point where its flavor is practically non-existent. In Russia vodka is usually served neat with plates of caviar as a bracing appetizer and some Americans like to follow this custom. However, most hosts and hostesses in this country prefer to serve a vodka Martini, Bloody Mary (vodka, tomato juice and condiments) or some other mixed drink, when vodka is the principal ingredient.

Vodka is the only spirit that does not lend itself to use as a cooking aid, for the obvious reason that it really has no flavor of its own.

Rum

Rum is one of the most varied and versatile of liquors. There are many kinds, ranging in color from pale to dark, any one of which can be used in these recipes, but remember that 86 to 90 proof rums are best for culinary purposes. They can be put to work in wonderful ways, including a variety of desserts, and offer a range of tastes—dry, smoky, heavy or pungent. Principally produced in tropical climes, such as the West Indies, from the fermented juice of sugar cane, molasses or by-products of sugar manufacture, rums from Cuba, Puerto Rico, Barbados, Trinidad, Martinique, Haiti and Jamaica offer rich flavoring both for drinks and dishes, from specially-flavored coffees to delectable *babas*.

For recipes that take advantage of the singular flavor of rum see those listed below. Use either light or dark rum, unless otherwise indicated.

Brunch, Luncheon, and Buffet Dishes
   Baked German Pancakes
Entrées
   Puerto Rican Chicken
Cakes and Cookies
   Baba au Rhum
   Babka
   Crowning Glory
   Chocolate Rum Chips
   Gingerbread
   Jamaican Date and Nut Bread
   Poncino Bars à la Caruba
   Porcupine Cake
   Rumbas
   Zuppa Inglese Cake
Desserts
   Bananas al Cordial
   Banana Soufflé Flambé
   Chocolate-Rum Mousse

Eggnog Chiffon Pie
Fruit Timbale
Kestane Sekeri
Pumpkin Rum Soufflé

BEER

Beer is not, of course, a wine and neither is it a spirit in the true sense of the word, since it is not distilled, rather being fermented from malt (or malt substitutes) and flavored with hops. However, the superb flavor it imparts, when it is used as one of the ingredients in certain dishes, merits one's consideration in the never-ending search for new and intriguing flavors.

Beer is one of mankind's oldest drinks and varies in color and character from the very pale and delicate to the dark and full-flavored. Babylonians, Egyptians and Greeks all made beer and Roman soldiers found this brew in the most remote corners of their far-flung empire. The first true dry beer came to America with German immigrants, but a rather flat beer, less dry and less refined, had been a staple colonial beverage from the time of the early Massachusetts settlements. Continental soldiers were allotted a daily beer ration. Colonial housewives cooked with beer and ale to add zest to their meat, fish and cheese dishes and, since beer acts as a leavening agent, it was frequently used in the making of breads and cakes.

Included in this book are a variety of recipes wherein beer plays an important role (see list below). You will find that it imparts a unique and delightful flavor.

Brunch, Luncheon and Buffet Dishes
  Chartreuse Pancakes
Entrées
  Beef and Beer Stew
  Fish Poached in Beer
  Lobster and Shrimp Bahas
  Sauerbraten

Breads
    Banana Bread
    Beer Bread
Cakes
    German Beer Cake

Scotch, Rye and Bourbon

For a dash of robust flavor, smoky or mellow, the liquors used in making highballs and cocktails will also provide new zest for a variety of dishes, from pâtés to desserts, all of which gain by the addition of a touch of whiskey. Various spirits distilled from grains are used by imaginative hostesses in many ways. Bisques and cream soups with a seafood base may be enhanced by a teaspoon or two of Scotch, and corn, clam and thick chicken soups by a dash of bourbon. These spirits can also be blended with syrups and used to heighten natural flavors in fresh and cooked fruit dishes.

Here, then, are some recipes that call for a "wee doch-an-dorrach."

Appetizers
    Ham and Bourbon Balls
    Roquefort and Whiskey Spread
Brunch, Luncheon and Buffet Dishes
    Scotch Omelet
    Scottish Lobster
Entrées
    Saddle of Venison with Bourbon
Cakes
    Happy Apple Cake
    Southern Belle Sponge Roll

Appetizers and Hors D'Oeuvres

Caviar and Egg Mousse

Wine used:
  Sherry

Accompaniment:
  Sherry

1 tbsp. unflavored gelatin	1 tsp. anchovy paste
2 tbsps. sherry	1 tsp. Worcestershire sauce
2 tbsps. lemon juice	pinch onion powder
6 hard-cooked eggs	1 2½-oz. jar Danish caviar
1 cup mayonnaise	ripe olives for garnish

Dissolve gelatin in sherry and lemon juice in a small bowl. Place bowl over water in a small pan or double-boiler and heat until gelatin is liquefied. Put eggs through a ricer or coarse strainer, add rest of ingredients except caviar and combine with gelatin. Lastly, add caviar and mix (just 2 or 3 strokes). A "clean" caviar (one with very little "ink") should be used. Danish caviar seems to have the least.

Place mixture in a greased mold and chill in refrigerator until ready to serve. Turn out on a platter. If ring mold is used, fill center with very large ripe olives.

An excellent buffet dish as well as an appetizer.

Chinese Egg Rolls

Wine used:
 Sherry

Batter:
2 eggs, beaten
1 cup flour, sifted
½ tsp. salt
1 cup water

Filling:
2 tbsps. shredded carrot
2 tbsps. shredded celery
2 tbsps. sherry
1 tbsp. finely chopped scallions or onions
½ cup chopped chicken or beef
Pinch pepper
1 tbsp. peanut oil
1 tbsp. sugar

To make batter, combine all ingredients. Heat skillet over medium heat and pour in about 3 tbsps. batter to make a very thin pancake. Cook one minute on one side only. Set aside until all pancakes are cooked, reserving a bit of the batter to seal the rolls.

To make filling, combine all ingredients. Put 1 tbsp. filling in the center of each pancake, fold in the sides, and roll forward. Seal the edges with the remaining batter brushed on with a pastry brush. Keep in refrigerator and when ready to serve, cook in a very large skillet with a tablespoon of peanut oil, turning when one side is brown. (Or deep-fry at 375°.) Serves 4.

Serve with chutney, Chinese mustard, preserved kumquats, soy sauce, or any other Oriental sauce.

Crabmeat and Bacon Balls

Wine used:
Dry sherry, Madeira or Málaga

1 lb. fresh crabmeat	1 cup dry bread crumbs
¼ tsp. dry mustard	Pinch salt
¼ cup dry sherry, Madeira, or Málaga	12 slices lean bacon
	3 tbsps. prepared mustard
1 cup mayonnaise	

In a large bowl place the crabmeat, dry mustard, wine, salt, and crumbs and mix well. Form into 24 small balls the size of a walnut. Wrap each ball with a half slice of lean bacon and secure with a wooden toothpick. Place on cookie sheets or broiler pans and broil 3 inches from flame for 10 minutes, turning once. Drain off fat and transfer to a platter. Keep warm in a 200° oven until ready to serve.

Serve with a mustard sauce made by combining the prepared mustard and mayonnaise.

Ham and Bourbon Balls

Spirit used:
Bourbon

6 hard-cooked eggs, chopped	Pinch of pepper
1 tbsp. minced chives or onion	3 tbsps. bourbon
1 cup ground, cooked ham	½ cup ground pecans or walnuts

In a medium-sized bowl, mix all the ingredients except the nuts, mashing well to get a smooth consistency. Roll into balls the size of a nickel. Place the ground nuts in a small bowl, add the balls a few at a time and toss lightly. Insert a toothpick in each ball and place on trays in refrigerator until ready to serve. Makes 36 balls.

Helvetia Fondue

Wine and Spirit used:
Neuchâtel, Kirsch

Accompaniment:
Neuchâtel

1 clove garlic	Pinch nutmeg
1 cup Neuchâtel	salt and pepper
1 lb. imported Swiss cheese*	¼ cup kirsch
3 tbsps. flour	French bread or dark rye bread

Rub the inside of an earthenware casserole or special fondue dish (see pages 7 to 9) with a clove of garlic and then discard the garlic. Place the casserole over a very low flame of the chafing dish heater and pour in 1 cup Neuchâtel. Heat the wine and with a wooden spoon gradually stir in the cheese, which has been coarsely grated, continuing to stir until blended. Stir in the flour, nutmeg, salt, pepper and kirsch. The fondue is ready to eat the minute all the ingredients are well blended. Eat directly from the casserole by spearing pieces of French bread or dark rye bread, broken into bite-size pieces, and dipping them into the fondue, swirling the bread around three times before popping it into your mouth. Serves 8.

This wonderful fondue can be served not only as an appetizer, but also as a Sunday night or after-the-theatre snack. If your bread drops from your fork and slips back into the dish, the forfeit is to pay for a round of drinks or kiss your dinner partner.

* Other Swiss fondue recipes call for various combinations of ripe and fresh Gruyère, Emmenthaler and Swiss cheeses.

Lobster Rumaki

Wine used:
  Sherry

1 pkg. frozen lobster tails
  (*approximately 3 to a box*)
¼ cup soy sauce
¼ cup sherry
1 can water chestnuts
12 slices lean bacon

Defrost lobster tails and shell. (To shell lobster tails easily, first cut membrane along both sides with kitchen shears.) Cut each tail into eight pieces. Marinate in soy sauce and sherry for half an hour. Combine each piece of lobster with a water chestnut, wrap in ½ slice of lean bacon and secure with a wooden toothpick. Broil 3 inches from flame until bacon is crisp, turning to make sure all sides are done. Makes 24 pieces.

Party Pinwheels

Wine used:
Sherry

Filling:
6 flat anchovies, chopped	2 tbsps. tomato sauce
1 can tuna fish	¼ tsp. Tabasco
1 tbsp. lemon juice	½ tsp. dry mustard
2 tbsps. sherry	

Pastry:
1½ cups flour, sifted	¼ cup shortening
pinch salt	¼ cup butter
½ cup ice water	

Preheat oven to 425°. Mix filling ingredients together. Blend pastry ingredients to form firm dough, roll out and cover with filling. Roll up jelly roll fashion in rolls 1 inch in diameter, slice, and bake on cookie sheets for 15 minutes. Makes 36.

A cocktail party must. If things go around it's the drinks, not the pinwheels.

Roquefort and Whiskey Spread

Spirit used:
Whiskey

½ lb. Roquefort cheese	½ lb. cream cheese
½ cup whiskey	

Combine the cheeses and add the whiskey slowly to bind the cheeses together. (Use more or less whiskey according to how it is absorbed by the cheeses.) Place in covered container in refrigerator. Will keep for months. Serves 24.

Shrimps in Sherry

Wine used:
Sherry

24 fresh shrimp	1 clove garlic, pressed
¼ cup sherry	1 tbsp. peanut or corn oil
1 tsp. powdered ginger	¼ cup soy sauce

Peel and de-vein shrimp and dry well. Marinate them in sherry, ginger, oil, soy sauce and garlic for approximately one hour. Cook shrimps and some of the marinade in top of chafing dish, electric skillet at 350°, or ordinary skillet over medium heat, for 5 minutes or until they turn pink or "blush." Serve with toothpicks.

A hidden persuader for delicate appetites.

Soups

Bouillabaisse à la Caen
(Simplified)

Wine used:
  Any dry white wine

Accompaniment:
  White Graves or California Semillon

½ cup olive oil
2 onions, sliced
1 clove garlic, pressed
1 carrot, chopped
1 lb. filet of sole
1 #2 can tomatoes
piece of bay leaf, pinch of salt, pepper, thyme, caraway seeds, Ac'cent

2 cups water
2 lobster tails
1 lb. fresh shrimp
½ tsp. dried saffron
2 pimentos, chopped
1 tbsp. lemon juice
1 cup dry white wine
12 minced clams

Put oil, onions, garlic and carrot in a 5-quart soup pot and cook until soft (approximately 5 minutes). Add the sole, cut in squares, tomatoes, bay leaf, thyme, caraway seeds, Ac'cent, salt and pepper to taste, and water. Simmer 20 minutes. Then add the shelled, raw lobster tails, cut in pieces, the shrimp, cut in thirds, and the shell of the lobster tails. Season with saffron and pimentos. Add lemon juice and wine and, lastly, the clams. (You will notice that the various seafoods are added according to the time required to cook them.) Bring to a boil and turn off heat.

To serve: Put slice of toasted French bread in each soup plate, add the Bouillabaisse and sprinkle with chopped parsley— or strain the broth, serve on slices of French bread in soup plates, and serve seafood separately on platter. Serves 6.

Only the eel has been eliminated from the original recipe and if you care to add it, you will have an authentic Bouillabaisse as served in Caen.

Cream of Cucumber Soup

Wine used:
Sherry

Accompaniment:
Chablis or Folle Blanche

2 cucumbers
4 tbsps. butter
3 tbsps. flour
1 quart milk

¼ cup sherry
1 cup chicken stock
¼ tsp. dill seeds
salt and white pepper

Wash the cucumbers and grate on a coarse grater. (Do not peel.) Sauté them in 2 tbsps. butter, keeping the flame low, until they are tender (about 10 minutes). Put in blender or through a coarse strainer.

In another pan, melt the remaining 2 tbsps. butter. Add flour away from the fire and blend until smooth. Add milk, sherry, chicken stock, dill seeds, salt and pepper. Cook and stir until it thickens; then add cucumber pulp and bring to a boil. Serve hot or cold. Serves 8.

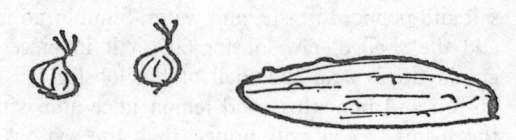

Cream of Watercress Soup

Wine used:
  Sherry

Accompaniment:
  Riesling

2 tbsps. butter
3 leeks, sliced
1 medium onion, chopped
3 medium potatoes, sliced
3 cups chicken stock
1 tsp. salt
1 cup milk
2 tbsps. sherry
1 bunch watercress

Melt butter in a 3-quart pot and slowly cook the leeks and onion in it. Add the potatoes, chicken stock and salt. Cook slowly for 30 minutes or until potatoes are tender. Mix in blender or force through a sieve and put back in pot. Add milk and sherry and stir well until smooth.

Wash watercress and dry on paper towels. Reserve some for garnish, discard heavy stalks from remainder and put in a 1-quart pot with a cup of water. Cook over a very high flame until it wilts. (This takes out the sharpness.) Drain the watercress and put through the blender set at high speed. When liquefied, add to soup and mix. Serves 6 to 8.

May be served hot—or cold, as a refreshing summer soup—on plates garnished with sprays of watercress.

French Onion Soup

Wine used:
  Dry white wine

Accompaniment:
  Graves, Chablis or Sauvignon Blanc

2 large Bermuda onions
2 tbsps. butter
1 tbsp. flour
2 quarts beef stock
½ cup dry white wine
2 tbsps. grated Parmesan cheese

Finely slice the onions, trying to keep the rings whole. This takes a bit of patience, but is worth the effort. Put onion rings and butter in a large pot and cook (stirring occasionally) over low heat until rings are soft and transparent. It will take 30 minutes to do this correctly, as it cannot be rushed. (This is the secret of a fine onion soup.) When soft, sprinkle the flour over the onions and gradually stir in the stock and the wine. Season to taste with salt and pepper, put back on the fire and simmer for 15 minutes more. Serve in soup bowls, garnish each bowl with a round of toasted French bread, and top with grated Parmesan cheese. May be put under the broiler for a moment or two, so that the cheese bubbles. Serves 8.

Perfect for wintry nights and after-ski.

Gazpacho

Wine used:
  Dry white wine

Accompaniment:
  Orvieto or Sauvignon Blanc

1 clove garlic
4 ripe tomatoes, quartered
1 small green pepper
1 small onion
1 peeled cucumber

1 tbsp. olive oil
½ cup dry white wine
½ tsp. paprika
¼ cup water
salt and pepper

Wash and prepare all vegetables and put through blender until smooth. Add rest of ingredients and chill until ready to serve.

Serve with side dishes of 1 cucumber, chopped fine; 1 hard-cooked egg, strained; chopped red and green peppers; and chopped onion—to be sprinkled over the soup. Serves 8.

Italian Holiday Soup with Meatballs

Wine used:
 Dry white wine

Accompaniment:
 Soave or Riesling

½ lb. ground chuck
2 eggs
3 tbsp. bread crumbs
Salt and pepper
½ cup dry white wine

Chopped parsley
Parmesan cheese
Chicken broth or beef broth
½ pkg. frozen green peas

Mix together chuck, 1 egg, bread crumbs, salt and pepper. Form into meat balls about the size of a marble. In the center of each put a tiny piece of parsley and a pinch of Parmesan cheese.

Heat chicken or beef broth and cook frozen peas in it for 5 minutes; add meat balls and cook for 5 minutes more, then add white wine. Stir in remaining egg, slightly beaten, just before serving. Serves 8.

Serve with Italian bread for meal-in-itself.

Minestra di Pasta e Fagioli
(Bean Soup with Vegetables)

Wine used:
 Dry red wine

Accompaniment:
 Valpolicella or Claret

½ lb. Turkish beans or white kidney beans
1 tbsp. oil
1 large onion, sliced
2 quarts beef stock
¼ cup dry red wine

½ cup celery, chopped
1 tbsp. tomato paste
1 carrot, chopped
½ lb. tubettini (fancy noodles)
salt and pepper

Soak beans overnight in a 5-quart pot in enough water to cover them. Next day drain off the water and keep beans aside. Cook oil and onion in the pot until onion is tender. Add rest of ingredients except tubettini. Cook gently for 30 minutes; then add tubettini and cook for 10 minutes more. Serves 8.

A thick soup and the mainstay of many Italian households—sometimes the whole meal with a salad and dessert to complete it.

Minestrone—Tuscan Style

Wine used:
  Dry red wine

Accompaniment:
  Bardolino or Pinot Noir

- 1 tbsp. poultry fat or oil
- 1 medium onion, chopped
- 1 tsp. parsley, chopped
- 1 tbsp. tomato paste
- 2 stalks celery, chopped
- 2 carrots, chopped
- 1 large potato, diced
- 1 cup fresh peas
- 1 zucchini, diced
- 1 cup shredded cabbage
- 1½ qts. beef stock
- ¼ cup dry red wine
- 1 tsp. salt
- 1 cup fancy pasta
- 1 tsp. chopped parsley
- bowl of grated Parmesan cheese

Place fat or oil in 5-quart soup pot. Add onions and parsley and cook until onion is soft. Add tomato paste followed by the vegetables, stock, salt, and lastly the wine. Cook uncovered over low heat for 45 minutes. Then add the pasta and cook 10 minutes.
Serve in deep soup plates with bowl of Parmesan cheese. Serves 8.

A hearty northern Italian dish that is made slightly differently in each province.

Mushroom Soup

Wine used:
  Sherry

Accompaniment:
  Barsac or Isle of St. George

- 1 medium onion, chopped
- 4 tbsps. butter
- ½ lb. fresh mushrooms, chopped
- 3 tbsps. flour
- 2 cups beef stock
- 2 cups milk
- ¼ cup sherry
- salt and pepper
- ¼ tsp. celery seed
- pinch Ac'cent

Sauté onion in 1 tbsp. butter until soft. Add mushrooms and cook for just one minute. In another pan put the remaining 3 tbsps. butter, and when melted, add the flour away from the fire. Add this to the onion mixture, pour in the beef stock and cook, while stirring, until smooth. Add the rest of the ingredients and cook for 5 minutes. For a smoother soup, pour into blender and blend for two minutes at low speed. Sprinkle each serving with paprika. Serves 8.

Simple, subtle and sublime.

Norwegian Lobster Bisque

Wine used:
  Sherry

Accompaniment:
  Alsatian Riesling or Pinot Blanc

1 pkg. lobster tails
3 cups chicken stock
piece bay leaf (size of dime)
2 tsps. salt
4 whole cloves
pinch allspice
pinch mace
white pepper
¼ cup uncooked rice
2 tbsps. butter
2 tbsps. flour
1 quart milk
2 egg yolks
¼ cup sherry

Simmer lobster, seasonings and rice in chicken stock for 20 minutes. Remove shells and let soup cool. In another pan melt the butter, add flour away from fire and blend until mixture is smooth. Add milk and egg yolks, put pan back on fire and cook until soup thickens a bit. Strain out cloves and bay leaf and mix bisque in blender until it is smooth and creamy. (If you do not have a blender, force bisque through a strainer.) Add sherry and correct the seasoning. Serves 8.

This is a very delicate bisque that differs from the American or French version as it does not have much color. The seasonings identify the country.

Norwegian Strawberry Soup

Wine used:
  Ruby port

Accompaniment:
  Rosé

1 cup boiling water
¼ tsp. salt
3 tbsps. tapioca
1 quart cold water
¼ cup sugar
1 quart whole fresh strawberries
¼ lemon, cut in slivers
2 cinnamon sticks
1 cup ruby port

Bring to a boil, in a 3-quart soup pot, 1 cup of water. Add

salt, slowly sprinkle in tapioca, and cook and stir for 5 minutes. Add the quart of cold water and stir until mixture reaches a boil again. Add sugar, strawberries, lemon and cinnamon sticks and simmer until fruit is soft (about 15 minutes). Remove from fire and add wine. May be served hot or cold. Serves 6 to 8.

If fresh strawberries are not available, use frozen berries and omit sugar.

Brunch, Luncheon and Buffet Dishes

Baked German Pancakes

Spirit used:
  Kirsch or rum

3 whole eggs	2 tbsps. melted butter
½ tsp. salt	red currant jelly
½ cup flour	cinnamon and sugar
½ cup milk	2 tbsps. kirsch or rum

Preheat oven to 450°. Break eggs into a medium size bowl. Beat with rotary beater for a minute or two, add the salt, flour and then milk, beating after each addition. Add 1 tbsp. of the melted butter. Grease a 10-inch pie plate with rest of melted butter, pour in batter, and bake for 10 minutes, then reduce oven heat to 400° and bake 20 minutes more. When crisp and brown, remove from oven; sprinkle with jelly, cinnamon and sugar; and flame with kirsch or rum. Serves 4.

This dish can also be served with coffee for a delightful Sunday night supper.

Beef and Vegetable Aspic

Wine used:
  Sherry

Accompaniment:
  Bordeaux or claret

3 tbsps. gelatin	Cold roast beef or pot roast
½ cup cold water	2 cups cooked vegetables or
3 cups beef stock	1 pkg. frozen mixed
¼ cup sherry	vegetables

If frozen vegetables are used, cook ahead of time and cool. Soften gelatin in cold water for 5 minutes in the bottom of a 4-quart bowl. Add boiling beef stock and sherry and blend well. Place a 1-quart mold in large bowl filled with ice cubes.

Be sure mold is level and surrounded by ice. Pour ½ cup of the stock mixture in the mold and turn mold until inside is coated. Arrange thin slices of meat around sides and on bottom to form a layer. Add more stock mixture, then a layer of vegetables, being careful not to disturb the meat. The food will chill as you work. Add more stock mixture and repeat with layers of meat and vegetables until they are all used and mold is filled. Aspic will be quite firm when you finish. Place in refrigerator until ready to serve.

To serve: Unmold on large platter and decorate with watercress or lettuce, quartered tomatoes and large ripe olives. Serve with mustard mayonnaise made by combining 3 tbsps. prepared mustard and 1 cup mayonnaise.

Chartreuse Pancakes

Spirits used:
Green chartreuse, yellow chartreuse, and beer.

Batter:
- 1 cup all-purpose flour
- 2 eggs
- 2 tbsps. lemon juice
- 1 tbsp. butter
- ¾ cup beer
- ¼ cup plus 2 tbsps. green chartreuse

Cream:
- 2 tbsps. melted butter
- 2 tbsps. lemon juice
- 2 tbsps. yellow chartreuse
- ¼ cup granulated sugar

Mix all batter ingredients in a small (6″) bowl, stirring briskly to incorporate. Set aside to mellow for about an hour. When ready to prepare, heat 1 tsp. butter in a small frying pan and add approximately 3 tbsps. batter to make a light pancake. Fry 1 minute on each side, remove from pan and set aside. Repeat with remaining batter (makes 12 pancakes). Mix together the cream ingredients and brush onto each pancake. Roll and place side by side on a heat-proof platter. Immediately before serving, reheat by placing the

platter under the broiler for 2 minutes. Flame at the table.
To flame: Place ¼ cup green chartreuse in a flaming ladle and ignite by tipping it toward the flame of a candle. Pour immediately over the pancakes, which in turn will ignite. Serve while still blazing. Serves 6 (2 pancakes each).

This recipe comes direct from the Carthusian Monks.

Duck Baroque

Wine used:
  Ruby port

Accompaniment:
  Beaujolais or Burgundy

1 5-6 lb. duck
2 tbsps. flour
½ cup ruby port
1 #2½ can bing cherries
1 tbsp. gelatin
¼ cup cold water
salt and white pepper

Wash and dry duck. Cook in an open roasting pan in 350° oven for about 2 hours or until tender. Remove from pan and cool. To the pan add flour, stir well, and then add wine and juice of the cherries (approximately 1 cup).
Soften gelatin in water and add to the sauce, season with salt and pepper, and cook, while stirring, until it thickens.
Remove skin, slice duck, and arrange slices in a deep serving dish. Pour the sauce over the duck and decorate with cherries. Chill in refrigerator until sauce is firm. Yields approximately 24 to 30 slices according to thickness.

This may be served in the dish in which it is prepared. It is particularly good as a buffet dish, as the slices come away nicely with some of the jellied sauce and cherries.

Lobster Supreme

Wine used:
Vermouth

Accompaniment:
Beaujolais Blanc or Chablis

3 tbsps. butter
3 tbsps. flour
salt and ground white
  peppercorns
1 cup milk
½ cup Parmesan cheese
¼ cup dry vermouth

¼ cup blanched, slivered
  almonds
2 tablespoons chopped
  parsley
pinch dried tarragon
pinch dried chives
1 lb. lobster meat (fresh, or
  frozen tails)

Cut lobster in bite-sized pieces. Melt the butter in the top pan of a chafing dish, remove from flame and add flour, salt and pepper to taste, and milk. Put back on fire and stir until sauce thickens a bit. Then add rest of ingredients and cook while stirring until lobster is heated through (approximately 5 minutes). Sprinkle generously with more parsley and chives and serve on toast points. Serves 4 to 6.

Pâté de Foie Gras en Aspic

Wine and spirit used:
Sherry or Madeira and brandy

Accompaniment:
Sherry or Madeira

½ lb. goose livers
  (or chicken livers)
1 tbsp. butter or chicken fat
2 eggs, hard-cooked
salt and pepper

4 tbsps. gelatin
¾ cup cold water
3 cups chicken stock
¼ cup sherry or Madeira
1 tbsp. brandy

Truffles

Pâté de foie gras: Sauté livers in butter or chicken fat until well cooked (approximately 10 minutes.) Put through food chopper and combine with mashed yolks of hard-cooked eggs, salt and pepper. Makes 1 cup. (You may, of course, prefer to buy your pâté de foie gras already prepared.)

Chicken Aspic: Soften 3 tbsps. gelatin in ½ cup cold water for 5 minutes in large bowl. Add boiling chicken stock and sherry or Madeira and mix well. Set 1-quart greased ring mold in large bowl that is filled with ice cubes. Make sure that mold is level and surrounded by ice. Decorate bottom of mold with tiny cut-outs of sliced truffles and sliced hard-cooked egg whites. Spoon 1 tbsp. aspic over the decorations, being careful not to float them. The aspic will congeal on contact. Pour more aspic into mold until it is one-half inch deep.

Soften remaining tbsp. of gelatin in remaining ¼ cup cold water for 5 minutes; then heat it in order to liquefy it. Pour over the pâté de foie gras, add brandy and mix well.

Put pâté de foie gras into a pastry bag with a #5 star tube and form a ring by squeezing the pâté out of the bag, directly onto the top of the hardened aspic. Carefully add rest of aspic, by tablespoonfuls, around the ring of foie gras, being careful not to disturb it. Aspic will become firm as it touches the mold. Leave the mold in the bowl of ice cubes until aspic is firm enough to move to refrigerator.

To serve: Unmold and decorate with sprays of watercress or parsley; or garnish with tomato wedges, black olives, potato salad and quartered hard-cooked eggs.

An unusual "conversation piece" which may also be served on slices of party rye bread as an appetizer. (36 slices)

Scotch Omelet

Spirit used:
  Scotch

3 eggs	1 tbsp. unsalted butter
1 tbsp. water	crushed macaroons
	2 tbsps. Scotch

Beat eggs with water, using rotary beater. In a 6-inch omelet pan or small pan with rounded sides, melt butter and when sizzling, pour in eggs. Stir while cooking over low heat, and when firm, fold over and turn out onto a plate. Sprinkle crushed macaroons on the top; then heat Scotch, pour over omelet, and flame. Serves 1.

Scottish Lobster

Spirit used:
  Scotch

Accompaniment:
  Muscadet or an American dry white wine

2 small lobsters
2 tbsps. butter
1 shallot or tiny onion, minced

½ cup heavy cream
1 tsp. tomato paste
¼ cup Scotch

Boil lobsters and extract meat when they have cooled. Cut into bite-sized pieces. Melt butter in top pan of chafing dish, add shallot or onion and stir until it is wilted. Add cream and tomato paste and stir well. Add lobster meat and cook until it is heated through (approximately 10 minutes), stirring to keep from sticking. When ready to serve, heat the Scotch in a flamer, pour over lobster and flame. Serve with toast points or white rice. Serves 6.

Shrimp Aspic

Wine used:
  Dry sherry

Accompaniment:
  Dry sherry

3 tbsps. gelatin
2¾ cups chicken stock
¼ cup sherry
1 cup mayonnaise

1 lb. cold cooked shrimp
1 cup cooked asparagus tips
salt and pepper
1 cucumber, unpeeled

ripe olives and hard-cooked eggs for garnish

Soften 2½ tbsps. gelatin in ½ cup cold stock. Heat 2 cups stock and add softened gelatin. Mix thoroughly and cool in refrigerator. Soften remaining ½ tbsp. gelatin in ¼ cup cold stock and place over hot water until dissolved. Cool this small amount, add the mayonnaise and set in refrigerator until mold is prepared.

Place quart mold in large bowl filled with ice cubes. This will chill the mold and the aspic will thicken as you work. Coat the bottom of the mold with a layer of gelatin and stock mixture. Then add shrimps, asparagus and cucumber in that order and in layers, alternating each layer of vegetables with a layer of gelatin mixture. Top with the cooled mayonnaise and gelatin mixture. Mold should be filled to the top. Chill until ready to serve. Turn out on a large platter and garnish with cucumber rings, ripe olives and hard-cooked egg slices. Serves 8 to 10.

Tongue à la Duchess of Windsor

Wine used:
  Sherry

Accompaniment:
  Bordeaux Rouge or Claret

- 1 3-3½ lb. smoked beef tongue
- 1 cup cooked and strained cranberries
- ½ cup dark brown sugar
- 12 whole cloves
- ¼ cup sherry
- ½ lemon, thinly sliced

Wash tongue well, cover with cold water in a 5-quart pot, bring to a boil and simmer covered over medium heat for 3 or 4 hours or until tender. When cooked, remove skin while still hot and when cool, cut off back part (or roots) of tongue. (This piece makes an excellent flavoring for split-pea soup.)
Sauce: Mix sugar, cranberries, cloves and sherry in chafing dish or large skillet. Simmer for 5 minutes. Add paper-thin slices of lemon and thinly sliced tongue and keep warm over low heat.

An excellent dish for buffet suppers, as it can be kept warm in the chafing dish. Also, it can be made days ahead of time.

Entrées—Seafood

Baked Shrimp Casserole

Wine used:
 Dry sherry

Accompaniment:
 Rosatelli or New York State Siebel Rosé

- 1 small white onion, minced
- 2 tbsps. butter
- ½ lb. fresh mushrooms, sliced
- 1½ cups canned tomatoes
- ½ cup light cream
- 2 tbsps. flour
- ¼ cup dry sherry
- 1 lb. fresh raw shrimps
- 1 tsp. Worcestershire sauce
- ¼ tsp. paprika
- ¼ tsp. thyme
- salt and white pepper
- ½ cup dry bread crumbs
- ¼ cup grated Parmesan cheese

In a 3-quart pot simmer onion in butter until it turns golden. Add the mushrooms and toss one minute. Add tomatoes and simmer for 10 minutes. Then stir in cream and sprinkle flour over this, stirring until it disappears. Add sherry, cleaned shrimps and seasonings. Pour mixture into a 1-quart casserole and sprinkle bread crumbs on top. Dot with butter and Parmesan cheese. Bake in a 400° oven for 20 minutes. Serves 4 to 6.

Filet of Sole Cordova

Wine and Spirit used:
Orange liqueur, sherry

Accompaniment:
Chilean Riesling or Delaware

- 2 tbsps. olive oil
- 2 onions, minced
- ½ lb. fresh mushrooms, sliced
- salt and white pepper
- ¼ tsp. soy sauce
- 4 filets of sole or flounder (approximately 1½ lbs.)
- pinch Ac'cent
- pinch paprika
- ½ cup sherry
- ¼ cup orange juice
- ½ cup orange liqueur
- 2 tbsps. fresh parsley, chopped

Preheat oven to 375°. Put olive oil in bottom of baking dish, 13 x 6 x 2 inches, and cover with half the onions, half the mushrooms and salt and pepper. Sprinkle with soy sauce. Add the filets in a layer and then the rest of the onions and mushrooms, seasoning, sherry, orange juice and ¼ cup of the liqueur. Bake uncovered for approximately 40 minutes or until the top of the fish is golden brown. Sprinkle with parsley.

To serve: Bring fish in the same dish to the table and flame with remaining ¼ cup of orange liqueur.

An interesting pyrotechnical display that tastes as good as it looks.

Filet of Sole Dugleré

Wine used:
  Dry white wine

Accompaniment:
  White Côtes du Rhone or Pinot Chardonnay

4 filets of sole
juice of ¼ lemon
4 medium-sized ripe tomatoes
3 tbsps. butter
¼ cup minced onion

2 tbsps. chopped parsley
2 tbsps. chopped chives
salt and cayenne pepper
½ cup dry white wine
2 tbsps. flour
¼ cup heavy cream

Preheat oven to 400°. Wash fish, sprinkle with lemon juice and pat dry with paper towels. Peel tomatoes, core and chop. Melt 1 tbsp. butter in a small pan, add onions and tomatoes and cook until both are soft (about 5 minutes). While these are cooking, cut fish lengthwise and roll each strip into a pinwheel. Secure with toothpick and place in a greased baking dish. Pour tomato and onion mixture over the fish, add half of the parsley and the chives, salt, pepper and white wine. Cover with waxed paper or aluminum foil. Bake for approximately 20 minutes.

Sauce: While fish is baking, melt the remaining 2 tbsps. butter in a 1-quart pan. Remove from fire, add flour, and mix well. When fish is cooked, place on a deep serving platter and keep warm in oven. Combine 1 cup of juice left in pan with flour and butter mixture, add cream and simmer until sauce is thick.

When ready to serve, remove sole from oven, pour sauce over and sprinkle with remaining parsley. Serves 4. (May be served cold.)

Filet of Sole Joinville

Wine used:
　Dry white wine

Accompaniment:
　Vouvray or Niagara

8-10 *small filets of sole*
½ *lb. fresh salmon*
juice of ½ lemon

2 *egg whites*
½ *cup light cream*
1 *tsp. salt*
½ *tsp. white pepper*

Preheat oven to 350°. Wash both the sole and salmon in water and sprinkle with lemon juice. Dry well with paper towels and set aside. Grind salmon coarsely in a blender or meat-grinder. Place in a small bowl, add the stiffly beaten egg whites, cream and seasonings.

Grease a 1-quart ring mold with 1 tsp. butter and line with the filets, light side down, and placed so that the narrow end of each filet is toward the center of the mold and the wide end is toward the outer rim, the ends of the filets extending over the inner and outer rims. Spoon salmon mixture into center of the filets and first fold the wide ends of filets over and then the narrow ends, thus encasing the salmon filling. Cover mold with a large square of waxed paper and tie with string. Place mold in 1 inch of water in a shallow pan and bake 30 minutes or until the fish is firm. Remove from oven and invert on a deep, ovenproof serving platter. Keep warm in oven while preparing sauce.

Sauce:

2 *tbsps. butter*
2 *tbsps. flour*
½ *cup juice (left in ring mold)*

2 *tbsps. heavy cream*
¼ *cup white wine*
salt and white pepper

Melt butter in a 1-quart pan, add flour and stir. Then add the juice of the fish, cream, white wine, salt and pepper. Cook and stir until smooth and thick and pour over filets. (The center of the ring can be filled with peas, sautéed mushrooms, or cucumbers cut in cubes and lightly sautéed in butter.) Serves 8.

When the mold is cut in portions, each has a pink center and a white edge.

Filet of Sole Marguery

Wine used:
  Dry white wine

Accompaniment:
  Pouilly-Fumé or Pinot Blanc

1½ lbs. filet of sole
½ cup dry white wine
piece of bay leaf (size of dime)
1 tsp. onion powder

salt and white pepper
1 doz. mussels
½ lb. shrimps
⅛ lb. butter
2 tbsps. flour

2 tbsps. light cream or milk

Preheat oven to 350°. Wash and dry the filets and place in greased baking dish. Pour the white wine over the fish, add piece of bay leaf, onion powder, and salt and pepper. Cover dish with waxed paper or aluminum foil, tucking in the edges, and bake for 25 minutes or until fish is done. While fish is baking, wash the mussels very well and poach them by placing them in a flat pan over high heat for 3 minutes. Be sure to cover them tightly and they will open by themselves from the heat. Take out of pan, remove the "beard," which is the hairy substance next to the shell, and set them aside for the sauce. Wash the shrimps, cut in half lengthwise and cook in butter until they "blush"—about 5 minutes.
Sauce: Melt butter, add flour away from heat and mix well. Add 1 cup of the mussel juice and stir until smooth. Put back on the fire, add the cream or milk and let it come to a slow boil. Remove from heat and serve.

To serve: Arrange the sole on a deep oven-proof platter, scatter over the shrimps and mussels and pour the sauce on top. Place under broiler for a minute or two to reheat. Serves 4.

Filet of Sole Maroca

Wine used:
White wine and Muscatel or sweet sherry

Accompaniment:
Beaujolais Blanc or Grey Riesling

4 filets of sole
1 tbsp. lemon juice
1 tbsp. butter
½ cup white wine
2 tbsps. Muscatel or sweet sherry
salt and white pepper

Preheat oven to 350°. Wash and dry fish. Place in buttered glass baking dish, sprinkle with lemon juice and add wines and salt and pepper. Cover with a piece of waxed paper or aluminum foil and bake for 20 minutes. When fish are baked, remove from pan, reserving juice, and transfer to an ovenproof serving platter. Keep warm in oven while preparing sauce.

Sauce:

3 egg yolks
1 tbsp. tarragon vinegar
salt and pepper
2 tbsps. cream or milk
½ cup fresh seedless grapes
2 tomatoes

Pour the juice from the baking pan into a small saucepan and heat over a high flame to reduce to ¼ cup. (Watch it carefully or there will be nothing left in the pan.) When juice is reduced, put it in the top of a double-boiler and add egg yolks and other ingredients, except grapes and tomatoes. Cook while beating with a wire whisk until smooth and thick. Peel tomatoes, cut in half, and take out seeds and pulp, leaving only the shells. Cut in thin strips and add with the grapes at the moment the sauce thickens. They should not be cooked—just covered with the sauce. Pour over sole and place under broiler briefly to heat the fish and sauce thoroughly. Serves 4.

A dish that is as distinctive in appearance as it is in taste.

Filet of Sole Walewska

Wine used:
  White wine

Accompaniment:
  White Graves or Niagara

4 filets of sole or flounder
juice of ¼ lemon
2 tbsps. butter
1 small onion, chopped
2 slices white bread
pinch marjoram
pinch thyme
pinch caraway seeds
salt and white pepper
1 small can minced clams
4 slices truffles
pieces of cooked lobster tail (*optional*)

Preheat oven to 350°. Wash filets, squeeze lemon juice over them and dry well with paper towels. Cook butter and onion in a 1-quart pan until onion is soft (5 minutes). Remove pan from fire and add the bread softened in water and squeezed dry, the seasonings, and the drained can of clams. Mix well.

Place 2 tbsps. of the filling on each of the filets and roll up. Put filled fish in well-greased baking dish, 6 x 9 x 2 inches. Pour over white wine and bake for 25-30 minutes. Remove from the pan to a platter and keep warm in oven until sauce is prepared.

Sauce: Pour juice from baking dish into top of double-boiler. Add 2 egg yolks, 2 tbsps. butter, 2 tbsps. Parmesan cheese and beat with wire whisk until sauce is smooth and thick. (Add pieces of cooked lobster tail, if desired.) Pour sauce over filets and decorate with slice of truffle on center of each. Serves 4.

Fish Poached in Beer

Spirit used:
  Beer

Accompaniment:
  Beer or ale

- 1 can beer
- 1 carrot, sliced
- 1 onion, sliced
- 1 stalk celery, sliced
- 8 peppercorns
- 5 whole cloves
- piece bay leaf (size of dime)
- 4 large filets of sole or flounder
- 2 tbsps. butter
- 2 tbsps. flour
- salt and white pepper
- 2 egg yolks
- ¼ cup light cream or milk
- ¼ cup grated Parmesan cheese
- ½ cup grated Gruyère cheese
- 2 tbsps. fresh parsley, chopped

Pour beer into 10-inch skillet, let come to a boil, add vegetables and spices and simmer for 10 minutes. Arrange filets in stock and simmer for 10 to 15 minutes, according to thickness of fish. When fish is poached, transfer to baking dish and prepare sauce.

Sauce: Reduce juices in pan to 1 cup and strain. In small pan melt butter and remove from fire. Add flour, mix, and then add salt and pepper, egg yolks and milk. Stir until smooth, put back on fire and blend in cheeses. When cheese is well blended, add fish stock and cook, while stirring, until smooth. Pour sauce over fish and broil until golden brown. Sprinkle with fresh chopped parsley and serve. Serves 4.

Lobster Cordon Bleu

Wine used:
Dry sherry

Accompaniment:
Pouilly-fuissé or Sauvignon Blanc

- 2 pkgs. lobster tails (frozen)
- 2 tbsps. olive oil
- 1 tbsp. finely chopped onion
- 4 egg yolks
- 1 cup cream
- 1 tbsp. tarragon vinegar
- ¼ cup sherry
- salt and cayenne pepper
- ¼ tsp. dry mustard
- 2 tbsps. grated Swiss cheese
- 3 tomatoes, skinned and sliced
- 2 tbsps. grated Parmesan cheese

In a large pot cook defrosted lobster tails in olive oil for 5 minutes or until they turn red. Take them out of the pan, cool, cut in pieces, and remove shells.

Sauce: Sauté onion. Put in the top of a double-boiler with egg yolks, cream, vinegar, sherry and seasonings. Stir until thick, add grated Swiss cheese, tomatoes and lobster and mix well. Pour mixture into a deep ovenproof serving dish. Sprinkle with Parmesan cheese and surround with Duchesse Potatoes (see p. 103). Brown under broiler and serve. Serves 4.

This is a satisfying one-dish meal and takes only about 30 minutes to prepare.

Lobster Flambé

Wine and spirit used:
  Cognac and white wine

Accompaniment:
  Pouilly-fumé or Sauterne

- 4 strips lean bacon
- 2 medium-sized onions, chopped
- 1 clove garlic, pressed
- ¼ lb. Prosciutto (or Westphalian ham)
- 1 pkg. lobster tails (approx. 1 lb.)
- ¼ cup Cognac
- ½ cup tomato sauce
- 1 tbsp. chopped parsley
- 1 cup white wine
- ¼ cup heavy cream

Chop bacon fine and put in cooking pan of a chafing dish. Cook and stir and when partly done, add onions. Continue to cook and stir, add garlic, and cook until onions are soft. Cut prosciutto or Westphalian ham into julienne strips and add to the pan. Add lobster tails which have been shelled and cut into 1-inch pieces and cook them until they turn pink. Flame with Cognac. Add tomato sauce, parsley and wine. Let simmer 5 or 10 minutes and lastly stir in cream. Mix well to heat through and serve over saffron or white rice. Serves 4.

Lobster à la Newburg

Wine and spirit used:
  Brandy and sherry, Marsala or Madeira

Accompaniment:
  Beaujolais Blanc or Sweet Semillon

1 lb. fresh lobster tails
4 tbsps. butter
¼ cup brandy
2 tbsps. flour
½ cup chicken stock

½ cup sherry, Madeira or Marsala
1 cup light cream
salt and white pepper
paprika

Shell lobster tails, cut in small pieces and sauté in 2 tbsps. butter until they turn pink (about 5 minutes). Flame them with brandy to clear them of any grease. Take out of the pan and set aside while preparing sauce.

Sauce: To liquid left in the pan add the remaining 2 tbsps. butter. When melted, add the flour, mix well and gradually add stock, half of the wine, the cream, salt and pepper. Cook, while stirring, until sauce is thick and smooth; then add remaining ¼ cup wine. Add pieces of lobster and toss them in the sauce until they are reheated. Sprinkle with paprika and serve over toast points. Serves 4.

If this dish is prepared in a chafing dish, make the sauce first, add the raw pieces of lobster after sauce is thickened, and cook for 5 or 6 minutes.

Lobster in Shells

Spirit used:
  Brandy

Accompaniment:
  Tavel or American Grenache Rosé

Shells:
1 ½ cups all-purpose flour
½ cup shortening and butter

pinch salt
½ cup ice water

Preheat oven to 375°. Place flour, salt, shortening and butter (half and half) in mixing bowl and with a pastry blender, work in fat quickly. Add the water bit by bit and keep tossing the dough in the bowl until it forms a solid ball. Turn dough out on a floured working area, separating it into two pieces, as it is easier to work with small portions. Roll out and cut into 3-inch rounds. Place rounds in deep muffin tins, press firmly, prick with fork, and bake for 20 minutes or until lightly browned. Remove and cool.

Filling:
- 2 tbsps. butter
- 1 tbsp. chopped onion
- 1 tbsp. chopped parsley
- 1 lb. lobster meat
- ¼ cup brandy
- ½ cup light cream
- 2 egg yolks
- Parmesan cheese
- Bread crumbs

Preheat oven to 375°. In a 1-quart pan melt the butter and sauté the onion and parsley until onion is tender. Stir in the lobster meat, cook a minute to heat through, then add brandy, cream, and egg yolks. Mix well and spoon the mixture by teaspoonfuls into the baked shells. Sprinkle with cheese and a few bread crumbs. Place in oven for just 10 minutes, until mixture becomes firm. Makes 2 dozen filled shells.

Lobster and Shrimp Bahas

Spirit used:
  Beer

Accompaniment:
  Beer

- 2 10-oz. pkgs. lobster tails
- 2 tbsps. butter
- 2 tbsps. flour
- 12-oz. can of beer
- ¼ cup sharp Cheddar cheese
- 1 tsp. dry mustard
- 1 tsp. salt
- 2 tbsps. Worcestershire sauce
- 1 lb. fresh shrimp

Defrost lobster tails, cut in pieces and remove shells. Melt butter in the upper pan of a chafing dish, add flour, and remove pan from the fire. Stir well, then add some of the beer

ENTRÉES—SEAFOOD

slowly, stir and put pan back over flame. Slowly add remaining beer and stir. Then add cheese, mustard, salt and Worcestershire sauce, stirring constantly with a wooden spoon or rubber scraper to keep sauce smooth. When sauce thickens add lobster and shrimp and cook for 5 minutes more, just enough to cook, but not toughen, them. Serve on toast points. Serves 8.

Mousseline de Crabe

Wine used:
  Sherry or dry Vermouth

Accompaniment:
  Barsac or Sauterne

3 tbsps. butter
1 lb. fresh crab meat
1 tbsp. grated onion
2 tbsps. chopped parsley
½ cup blanched, sliced almonds

¼ cup sherry or dry vermouth
salt and white pepper
1 cup Béchamel Sauce
½ cup heavy cream, whipped

In upper pan of a chafing dish, heat butter directly over the flame, add the crab meat and sauté for 2 minutes to heat it. Add the onion, almonds, sherry or vermouth, salt, pepper and half the parsley. Then mix in Béchamel Sauce and fold in whipped cream. When thoroughly heated, serve on toast points and sprinkle remaining parsley on top of each portion. Serves 6.

Oysters Madeira

Wine used:
  Madeira

Accompaniment:
  Madeira

3 tbsps. butter
pinch cayenne
1 tsp. dry mustard
½ tsp. dry tarragon
  or
1 tsp. tarragon vinegar

pinch salt
¼ lb. sliced fresh mushrooms
¼ cup diced celery
¼ cup Madeira
1 cup light cream
3 egg yolks

2 dozen fresh oysters

In upper pan of chafing dish, melt butter, add seasonings, celery, mushrooms and cook for 5 minutes or until celery is wilted, but not cooked through. Add cream, then egg yolks and beat with a wire whisk until they are incorporated. Add Madeira. When sauce is thick, add oysters and cook 3 to 5 minutes until they curl. Serve on toast points. Serves 4.

Oysters Royale

Wine used:
Sherry

Accompaniment:
Sherry

- 2 tbsps. butter
- 1 tsp. dry mustard
- 1 small can anchovies
- salt and ⅛ tsp. cayenne pepper
- 2 tbsps. flour

- 1 cup finely chopped celery
- 2 cups heavy cream
- ¼ cup sherry
- 2 dozen oysters
- paprika
- 1 lemon, thinly sliced

Place butter in upper pan of chafing dish, directly over the fire. Add mustard. Drain can of anchovies and add to the dish, stirring until they are incorporated into the sauce. Add salt and pepper and sprinkle on flour. Add celery and stir until it is heated. Add cream very slowly, then sherry. When sauce is hot, add the oysters and their juice and cook 3 to 5 minutes, or until they curl. Dust on paprika and serve on toast points or rice, with a slice of lemon on the side. Serves 4.

Paella

Wine used:
  Sherry

Accompaniment:
  Tavel Rosé or Mateus Rosé

¼ cup olive oil
1 3-lb. broiler chicken
¼ cup Spanish sherry (dry)
1 large onion, chopped
2 tbsps. butter
1 cup rice, washed
2 large cloves garlic
1 qt. chicken stock
1 lobster tail (approx. ½ lb.)
3 ozs. smoked Spanish or Italian sausage

½ lb. cleaned raw shrimp
3 slices canned pimento, cut in pieces
salt and pepper to taste
pinch chili powder
pinch Ac'cent
½ tsp. dried saffron steeped in 2 tbsps. hot water
8 cherrystone clams in shells
6 ripe olives, sliced

Preheat oven to 375°. Heat olive oil in 5-quart skillet and brown the chicken whole. Take out of pot and when cool enough to handle cut in 8 pieces and place in large 1½-quart casserole. Pour sherry on top. Sauté the onion in 2 tbsps. butter until golden (approximately 5 minutes) and pour over chicken pieces. Add the rice and the very finely chopped or pressed garlic, then half the heated chicken stock. Cover and bake for 40 minutes until the rice absorbs the stock. Add the lobster tail, cut in pieces and shelled, the sausage, shrimp, pimento pieces, seasonings to taste and the saffron and water. Add more stock, if needed. Cover again and bake for 25 minutes more. Remove casserole from oven, add clams and olives and return to oven for 10 more minutes or until clams open. Serve paella from same casserole in which it is baked, making sure that each serving contains some of each ingredient. Serves 4 generously.

A fantastically good one-dish company meal.

Shrimps Marinière

Wine used:
  Dry white wine and dry sherry

Accompaniment:
  Sweet Semillon or Badacsony

1¼ cups dry white wine
1 cup water
1 cup chicken stock
1 onion, minced
3 celery tops
3 sprigs parsley
½ tsp. caraway seeds
½ tsp. thyme
1½ lbs. raw shrimp, cleaned

2 tbsps. butter
2 tbsps. flour
juice ½ lemon
3 egg yolks
½ cup heavy cream
¼ cup sherry
1 tbsp. parsley
1 tsp. paprika
salt and pepper

In a 3-quart pot put 1 cup of the white wine, the water, chicken stock, onion, celery tops, parsley and seasonings and simmer for 15 minutes uncovered. Add shrimps and cook for just 5 minutes. Remove shrimps, strain stock and retain ¾ cup for sauce.

Sauce: In the top of a double-boiler put butter, flour, lemon juice, egg yolks, cream, salt and pepper. Stir until smooth, then turn up heat and stir in remaining ¼ cup white wine, sherry, parsley and paprika. Add salt and pepper and shrimp stock. Cook until mixture is thick, add shrimps, and reheat them in the sauce for about 5 minutes. Serve on toast points or saffron rice. Serves 8.

Shrimps Tempura

Wine used:
 Sherry

Accompaniment:
 Saki

1 lb. large fresh shrimp
1 cup flour

1 whole egg
½ cup water

Clean shrimp, de-vein and dry with paper towels. Make batter by combining flour, egg and water, dip shrimps in it and deep fry at 375° until they are golden brown and puffed (approximately 5 minutes). Serve with Tempura Sauce. Serves 4.

Tempura Sauce:
¼ cup soy sauce
¼ cup sherry
¼ cup water

1 tsp. sugar
¼ tsp. salt
¼ tsp. dry ginger

Mix in a small pot, bring to a boil and serve hot in separate bowl.

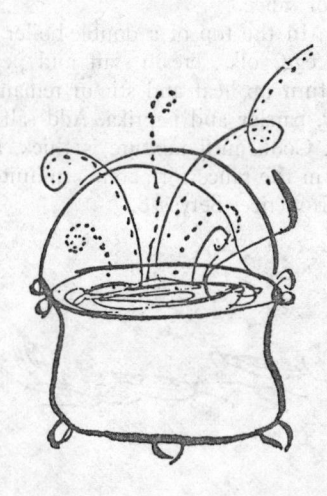

Entrées—Fowl

Canard Bigarade (Duckling with Orange)

Wines used:
  Sherry and red wine

Accompaniment:
  Hermitage or Pinot Noir

- 1 4-lb. duckling
- 1 tbsp. butter or oil
- 3 tbsps. sherry
- 1 clove garlic, crushed
- 2 large oranges
- 4 mushrooms, sliced
- 1 tbsp. potato starch
- 1 tsp. tomato paste
- pinch salt, pinch chili powder
- ¼ cup red wine
- 1 tbsp. red currant jelly
- 1½ cups light stock
- fresh parsley

Wash and dry duckling. Cut in 8 pieces and brown, skin side down, in butter or oil in large 10-inch skillet. Flame with sherry and remove the pieces from the pan.

To the pan add the garlic, shredded rind of one orange, mushrooms, potato starch, tomato paste, salt and chili powder. Mix, add orange juice and stock and stir over the fire until the sauce thickens. Add the wine and jelly and cook and stir for a minute. Add the pieces of duckling, cover pan and cook slowly until tender (approximately one hour).

To serve: Arrange the pieces of duckling in deep serving dish, add the peeled and seeded sections of one orange, sprinkle the top with fresh parsley and sauce from the pan. Serves 4.

Canard Maison (Duckling with Cherries)

Wines used:
  Brandy and Muscatel

Accompaniment:
  Pommard or Burgundy

½ cup candied cherries
½ cup Muscatel
1 4-lb. duckling
1 tbsp. butter or oil
3 tbsps. brandy
1 clove garlic, crushed
1 tbsp. potato starch

1½ cups chicken stock
5 mushrooms, quartered
1 tbsp. apple jelly
⅛ tsp. dill seed
salt and white pepper
chopped fresh parsley

Soak cherries in muscatel overnight. Wash duckling well and dry. Cut in eight pieces and brown quickly, skin side down, in heated butter or oil in 10-inch skillet. Flame with brandy and remove from pan. Add garlic, potato starch, mushrooms, cherries and the wine in which they have soaked. Then add 1½ cups chicken stock and stir over heat until thickened. Put back pieces of duck, and add jelly, dill seed, salt and pepper. Arrange pieces on a deep serving dish and pour over the sauce. Sprinkle with parsley and serve. Serves 4.

This dish may be prepared in the morning, left in the skillet and reheated for dinner. If you double the recipe, double everything except the stock. The juices of the extra duckling will compensate for the stock.

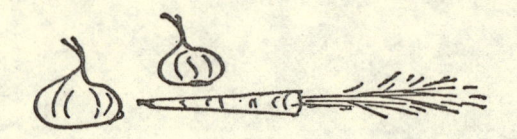

Capon au Champagne

Wine used:
Still champagne or other dry white wine

Accompaniment:
Champagne, Chablis or Semillon

- 3 tbsps. butter
- 1 4-5 lb. capon
- ½ cup chopped onions
- 3 chopped shallots
- 1 large clove garlic
- 6 fresh mushrooms, sliced
- dash nutmeg
- piece of bay leaf (size of dime)
- 2 cups still champagne (or other dry white wine)
- 1 tbsp. flour
- 4 egg yolks
- 1 cup light cream or milk
- salt and white pepper
- chopped truffles

Melt 2 tbsps. butter in large kettle, add capon and brown on all sides (5 minutes). Place on serving platter. Add to the kettle the onions and shallots and cook until they are soft. Add crushed garlic, mushrooms, nutmeg, bay leaf and champagne (or other white wine). Put capon back in pot, cover and cook until tender (approximately 45 minutes). Transfer bird to platter and keep warm.

Sauce: In a 1-quart pan melt the remaining tbsp. butter, add flour away from heat. Add first the egg yolks which have been beaten with the cream (or milk) and then the stock that is left in the pot. Keep sauce hot and when ready to serve pour over capon. Sprinkle with chopped truffles and serve with cooked noodles or rice. Serves 4.

Chicken with Almonds

Wine used:
  Dry white wine

Accompaniment:
  Argentine Riesling or Sauvignon Blanc

2 tbsps. butter or oil	2 cups chicken stock
½ cup drained, crushed pineapple	1 tsp. salt
2 tbsps. potato starch	½ cup sliced, toasted almonds
½ cup pineapple juice	½ cup thinly sliced pascal celery
½ cup dry white wine	

2 cups cooked chicken

Drain pineapple, reserving juice, and sauté in butter or oil for a minute or two until heated. Remove from fire and sprinkle on potato starch. Mix with a wooden spoon until pineapple and starch are blended. Then add pineapple juice, wine and chicken stock. Heat and stir until mixture thickens. Add remaining ingredients, heat well and serve over white rice. Serves 4.

A delectable chicken dish from Argentina.

Chicken Cacciatora Piemontese

Spirit used:
  Brandy

Accompaniment:
  Italian Bardolino or Pinot Noir

2 tbsps. dried Italian mushrooms	1 large clove garlic, pressed
1 cup hot water	½ cup green pepper
1 3½ lb. chicken	1 cup chopped onion
1 tbsp. olive oil	pinch basil
2 tbsps. brandy	pinch oregano
½ cup chopped celery	½ tsp. salt
	pinch cayenne pepper

½ cup Italian tomato sauce

Ahead of time wash mushrooms in a strainer and put in hot

water to soften (approximately 1 hour). Cut chicken in 8 serving pieces and brown quickly in oil. Flame with brandy and remove from pan. Add vegetables and seasonings to the pan; then softened mushrooms and water in which they are soaking, tomato sauce, and chicken pieces. Cover and cook until tender (approximately 45 minutes). Serve over rice or noodles.

Chicken Divan

Wine used:
  Sherry

Accompaniment:
  Montrachet or dry Sauvignon

1 5-lb. fowl
1 stalk celery
1 small onion
1 carrot
1 tsp. salt
1½ cups white sauce
  (see Béchamel)
¼ tsp. nutmeg

½ cup Hollandaise sauce
½ cup heavy cream
  (whipped)
¼ cup sherry
½ tsp. Worcestershire sauce
2 pkgs. or 1 large bunch broccoli
1 cup grated Parmesan cheese

Put chicken in a large (5 quart) pot, add 2 quarts of water and bring to a boil. Add celery, onion, carrot, and salt and cover pot. Let simmer until tender (approximately 1 hour). Stock may be frozen for later use in other dishes.

While chicken is cooking, prepare the Béchamel sauce and put in large bowl and stir in the nutmeg. Make the Hollandaise Sauce, add to Béchamel, add whipped cream, sherry and Worcestershire. Place bowl in refrigerator.

If you are using frozen broccoli, put in large, flat, 10-inch skillet with 1 tbsp. butter and *nothing else*. Cover pan and cook slowly for 7 minutes until stalks are tender, but still bright green. If fresh broccoli is used, cook until just barely tender. When cooked, place on a large, deep, oven-proof serving platter. When chicken is cooled, remove the skin and slice meat. Lay the slices over the cooked broccoli and sprinkle over them some of the cheese, pour sauce over all and sprinkle again with the remaining cheese. Place dish under the broiler, 3 inches from flame, and cook, watching carefully, until the top is brown and bubbly (about 5 minutes or less). Serve immediately. Serves 6 to 8.

NOTE: *This may seem like a great deal of work, but much of it can be done ahead of time. The chicken can be cooked days in advance and kept in the refrigerator or frozen, and the sauces can be made in the morning of the day you serve the dish.*

Chicken and Gin on the Spit

Spirit used:
  Gin

Accompaniment:
  Alsatian Riesling or Moore's Diamond

2 broiler chickens
  (approx. 2 lbs. each)
½ cup gin

½ cup orange juice
¼ cup honey
¼ tsp. powdered ginger

Cut each chicken into 8 pieces and cover with marinade made by combining gin, orange juice, honey and ginger. After 1 or 2 hours remove chicken and either cook on an outdoor grill or broil in oven. Baste every 10 minutes with the remaining marinade. Serves 8.

Pork, ham or game birds may be substituted for chicken.

Chicken with Olives

Wines used:
 Sherry and dry white wine

Accompaniment:
 Verdicchio or Pinot Blanc

1 3½ lb. chicken
2 tbsps. olive oil
2 tbsps. sherry
2 tbsps. butter
2 tbsps. flour
salt and pepper
pinch basil

1 cup chicken stock
¼ cup dry white wine
12 ripe olives
1 pimento, diced
2 tbsps. chopped chives or parsley

Clean, wash and dry chicken. Cut in 8 pieces and brown in heated olive oil in large skillet. Flame with sherry and remove from pan.
Sauce: In the same skillet add butter, flour, salt, pepper and basil. Mix, add stock and white wine and blend until smooth. Cook sauce until it thickens and add chicken. Then cover pan and cook 45 minutes or until tender.
Just before serving add olives and diced pimento. Decorate with chopped chives or parsley and serve with cooked, wide noodles. Serves 4.

Coq au Vin

Wines and spirit used:
 Brandy, sherry, red wine and white wine

Accompaniment:
 Burgundy or claret

2 tbsps. butter or oil
1 4-lb. chicken
2 tbsps. brandy
2 tbsps. sherry
18 small white onions
5 fresh mushrooms
1 tbsp. guava jelly

1 tbsp. potato starch
½ cup red wine
¼ cup white wine
½ cup beef stock
pinch chervil (English parsley)
salt and white pepper

Heat butter or oil in large 10″ skillet and brown the whole

chicken in it. Flame first with brandy, then with sherry. Remove bird from pan, cut in 8 serving pieces and set aside until the gravy is prepared.
Gravy: To juices in pan add onions and sliced mushrooms and toss over fire for a minute. Take pan from fire and add potato starch. Mix well and gradually add red wine, white wine, beef stock and salt and pepper; then parsley and jelly. Place pan on fire, stir until gravy thickens, put back pieces of chicken, cover, cook for 45 minutes or until chicken is tender. Put in deep platter and sprinkle over some more fresh parsley. Good served with noodles or rice. Serves 4.

NOTE: *Red wine is the accompaniment since it is the most prominent wine in the coq au vin.*

Cornish Hen Plymouth

Wine and spirit used:
  Plymouth gin, and red wine

Accompaniment:
  Meursault or Burgundy

4 Cornish hens
  (approx. 1 lb. each)
fruit stuffing (see page 137)
2 tbsps. butter
5 tbsps. Plymouth gin
1 tsp. juniper berries, crushed
1 tbsp. potato starch
1 cup strong beef stock
pinch salt, pinch garlic
  powder, dill
¼ cup black currant jam
½ cup red wine

Stuff hens with fruit stuffing, tie and brown quickly in butter in large 10-inch skillet. Flame with 3 tbsps. gin and remove from pan.
Sauce: Add to the pan the crushed juniper berries, potato starch, stock, seasonings, and jam. Stir until smooth, add wine and stir again until smooth. Put the birds back in pan, cover and cook for 40 minutes or until tender.
To serve: Remove the birds from pan to large, deep platter. Pour over 2 tbsps. gin and flame at table. Serves 4.

Duck, chicken or turkey may be substituted for the Cornish hens.

Duckling Marengo

Wines used:
Marsala or Muscatel and Sauternes

Accompaniment:
Quincy or Sauvignon Blanc

1 4-lb. duckling	salt and white pepper
1 cup Sauternes	½ cup water
½ cup Marsala or Muscatel	½ tsp. celery seed
1 navel orange, sliced	½ tsp. marjoram
1 lemon, sliced	½ tsp. thyme
1 tbsp. olive oil	

Wash duckling and cut in quarters. Marinate at least 48 hours in refrigerator in sauce made by combining rest of ingredients. When ready to cook, remove and dry. Dredge in flour and brown in hot olive oil in large skillet.

To the pan add:
12 sweet pickled onions	1 tbsp. potato starch
8 mushroom caps	strained marinade

Cook covered over low heat for one hour or until duckling is tender.

To serve: Put pieces in deep, heat-proof serving dish and broil for a minute or two to crisp the skin. Pour over sauce and serve. Serves 4.

Crème de Volaille

Wine used:
 Sherry

Accompaniment:
 Chablis or Riesling

3 cups ground cooked chicken
¼ cup sherry
¾ cup dried bread crumbs
½ cup sliced fresh mushrooms
3 whole eggs
pinch sage
pinch thyme
salt and pepper
2 cups white sauce
1 tbsp. chopped parsley
1 hard-cooked egg

Preheat oven to 375°. Put pieces of left-over chicken through a coarse meat grinder, add sherry, bread crumbs, mushrooms, eggs, seasonings and sauce. Stir until ingredients are incorporated. Pour in buttered 1-quart casserole and bake for 25 minutes. Place on platter and garnish with chopped parsley and strained egg. Serves 4 to 6.

Duck Provençale

Wine and spirit used:
  Brandy and dry white wine

Accompaniment:
  Graves or Pinot Blanc

1 5-lb. duck	2 tbsps. chopped celery
1 tbsp. butter or oil	piece of bay leaf (size of dime)
2 tbsps. brandy	1 cup beef stock
1 tbsp. potato starch	24 stuffed green olives
2 tbsps. chopped parsley	¼ cup water

1 tbsp. chopped chives

Wash and dry duck and brown quickly in butter or oil in large skillet. Flame with brandy and remove from pan. To the pan add potato starch, mix well and then add parsley, celery, stock and seasonings. Stir until the sauce thickens and add wine. Put the duck back in pan, cover and cook for 1½ hours or until tender.

While duck is cooking, parboil olives in ¼ cup of water for 5 minutes to remove some of their salt. When the duck is tender, add olives to sauce and stir until they are coated.

To serve: Arrange duck on deep serving platter and pour sauce over it. Sprinkle with finely chopped olives. Serves 4.

Glazed Chicken Breasts

Wine used:
  Ruby port

Accompaniment:
  Riesling or Traminer

1 tbsp. butter	salt and white pepper
1 tbsp. potato starch	½ tsp. ground allspice
½ cup water	1 tbsp. Sauce Robert
¼ cup ruby port	(Escoffier) or
1 6-oz. jar red currant jelly	Worcestershire
juice of ½ lemon (2 tbsps.)	6 halves of chicken breasts

Preheat oven to 375°. Melt butter and potato starch and

mix well. Add rest of ingredients, except chicken breasts, and bring to a boil to dissolve jelly and incorporate flavors. Pour into open roasting pan and add chicken. Put in oven and baste every 15 minutes until breasts are tender and take on a rosy color. Add more wine if sauce becomes too thick. Serves 4.

Excellent served with wild rice.

Poulet en Casserole

Wine used:
  Sherry

Accompaniment:
  Pouilly-Fumé or Semillon

- 1 2-3 lb. chicken
- 2 tbsps. butter or oil
- 2 tbsps. sherry
- 12 small, white onions
- 6 pieces of carrots
- 6 pieces of yellow turnips
- 6 pieces celery
- 2 pieces leeks
- 5 fresh mushrooms, quartered
- 1 tsp. tomato paste
- 1 tbsp. potato starch
- 1 cup chicken stock
- ¼ cup white wine
- salt and pepper
- fresh chopped parsley

Wash and dry chicken. Brown whole in skillet in heated butter or oil, turning constantly to brown all over. Flame with sherry and remove from pan. Add to the pan the onions, carrot, turnip, celery, and leek pieces and toss. Add mushrooms, stir in tomato paste and potato starch. Pour in chicken stock and stir over fire until the sauce thickens. Add white wine, salt and pepper. Cut chicken in 8 pieces and put back in sauce. Cover and cook until tender (approximately 45 minutes). When ready to serve, arrange pieces of chicken in a deep serving platter, scatter vegetables on top, cover with sauce and sprinkle with chopped parsley. Serves 4.

NOTE: *This is an excellent company dish, as it can be made in the morning or even the day before, if necessary. It should be light in color and the sauce transparent to show the colors of the vegetables.*

In doubling the recipe, double everything but the stock as the juices of the chicken will take the place of an additional cup of stock.

Puerto Rican Chicken

Spirit used:
  Puerto Rican rum, light or dark

Accompaniment:
  Bordeaux Blanc or Sauterne

1 3½-lb. chicken
3 tbsps. soy sauce
½ cup honey
¼ cup Puerto Rican rum
2 garlic cloves, crushed
1 egg yolk
½ cup chicken stock
1 jar preserved ginger

Have butcher cut the chicken in eight pieces, eliminating back bone. Cut off wing tips and discard or use with back bones for stock. Preheat oven to 375° for 10 minutes. Wash chicken and pat dry. Put in pan and cover with sauce made by combining soy sauce, honey, rum, garlic, egg yolk, chicken stock and ¼ cup syrup from jar of preserved ginger. Bake for 45-60 minutes, basting every 15 minutes. When tender, remove from pan to heated platter and sprinkle with pieces of preserved ginger. Serves 4.

Entrées—Meat

Austrian Pot Roast with Horseradish

Wine used:
  Dry white wine

Accompaniment:
  Traminer or Pinot Blanc

1 tbsp. oil or butter
2 lbs. boned rump roast or shoulder of beef
6 medium onions, sliced in thin rings
2 tbsps. flour
1 6-oz. bottle prepared horseradish
1 clove garlic, pressed
¼ cup white table wine
salt and pepper
1 tbsp. sugar

Heat oil in 10-inch skillet and brown meat quickly to seal in the juices. Remove from the pan until sauce is prepared. To the pan add sliced onions and cook for 5 minutes or until they take on a bit of color. Sprinkle with flour and add horseradish, garlic, wine, sugar, and salt and pepper. Mix well, put meat back into pan and cook it over a low fire until tender (approximately 1 hour).

To serve: Cut the meat in long, even slices and cover it with the sauce from the pan. Serve hot with mashed potatoes or broad noodles, buttered and sprinkled with caraway seeds. Serves 4.

Baked Western Steak

Wine used:
  Red wine

Accompaniment:
  Reserve Ducale or claret

1 3½-lb. sirloin steak
pinch garlic
salt and cayenne pepper
1 tsp. prepared mustard
¼ cup red wine
½ cup water
½ cup tomato sauce
1 onion, thinly sliced

Season the steak with garlic, salt, pepper and mustard and let mellow for at least 30 minutes. Preheat oven to 350°.

Choose a roasting pan that is about 12 x 9 x 3 inches and put in it the wine, water, tomato sauce and onion and steak. Bake for 30 minutes or until steak is cooked to the proper degree of "doneness" (about 30 minutes for rare meat and about 40 minutes for medium, depending on thickness of steak. Use oven thermometer for best results). Serves 6.

This is a wonderful company dish, as it can be prepared well in advance and baked at the last minute.

Barbecued Potted Beef

Wine used:
  Red wine

Accompaniment:
  American red wine or Italian Chianti

- 2 lbs. chuck or cross rib roast
- 1 tbsp. oil
- 3 medium onions, sliced thinly
- ¼ cup red wine
- ½ cup tomato sauce
- 2 cloves garlic, pressed
- 2 tbsps. dark brown sugar
- ½ tsp. dry mustard
- 1 tbsp. lemon juice
- ¼ cup catsup
- ¼ cup cider vinegar
- 1 tbsp. Escoffier sauce (Robert)

Brown the meat whole on both sides in hot oil in large skillet. Add rest of ingredients, replace meat, cover and cook slowly for 1 hour or until tender. Serves 4.

NOTE: *To avoid having thin, watery gravy, remove cover occasionally, invert quickly and discard accumulated condensed steam.*

Beef and Beer Stew

Spirit used:
  Beer

Accompaniment:
  Beer

1½ to 2 lbs. chuck roast
1 tbsp. butter
3 diced onions
1 clove garlic, crushed
1 can peeled tomatoes (#1½)
1 tbsp. paprika
pinch cayenne pepper
pinch salt
1 cup beer
4 large potatoes

Cut meat in 1½-inch squares and remove fat. Heat butter in skillet and brown meat quickly to retain juices. Add onions, garlic, tomatoes and other seasonings—then the beer. Cover and cook for 45 minutes or until meat is tender. Peel potatoes and using special scoop, make into 24-30 balls. Fifteen minutes before serving stew, add potato balls and cook until done. Serve in deep platter. Serves 4.

Another contribution from England's collection of fine recipes.

Benlose Fugle (Danish Veal Rolls)

Wine used:
  White wine

Accompaniment:
  Beaujolais or Pinot Blanc

1 lb. veal cutlets (six pieces)
bread stuffing*
2 tbsps. butter or oil
5 fresh mushrooms, sliced
1 tbsp. flour
¼ cup beef stock
¼ cup white wine
pinch dill seeds or fresh dill
salt and pepper

Pound the veal cutlet pieces very thin (see p. 11). Stuff and roll, tie with string at each end and brown quickly in hot butter or oil. Remove the meat from the pan and put in mushrooms, flour, beef stock, wine, dill seeds, salt and pep-

per. Put veal back in pan, cover and cook until tender (approximately 45 minutes).
* *Bread stuffing:* Sauté ½ onion, chopped, and ½ stalk of celery, chopped, in 1 tbsp. butter until tender. Add salt, pepper, pinch thyme, pinch sage, and two slices of white bread dipped in water and squeezed dry.

Boeuf à la Bourguignonne

Wine and spirit used:
  Burgundy and brandy

Accompaniment:
  Burgundy

- 2 lbs. beef (chuck or round)
- 2 tbsps. butter
- 3 tbsps. brandy
- 12 small, white onions
- 5 fresh mushrooms
- 1 tbsp. tomato sauce

- 3 tbsps. flour
- 1½ cups beef stock
- ¾ cup Burgundy
- 1 tbsp. red currant jelly
- piece bay leaf (size of dime)
- salt and pepper

Cut beef into 2-inch squares and brown quickly in 1 tbsp. butter in large skillet. Flame with brandy and remove from pan.
Sauce: Melt the remaining tbsp. butter in pan and add onions, mushrooms cut in quarters, tomato sauce, and flour. Mix. Add beef stock, ½ cup of the wine, jelly, bay leaf, and salt and pepper to taste. Put the meat back in pan, cover and cook until tender (approximately 45 minutes). Just before serving add remaining ¼ cup Burgundy. Serves 4.

An ode to joie de vivre.

Braciola (Rolled Beef with Red Wine)

Wine and spirit used:
Red wine and brandy

Accompaniment:
Bardolino or Burgundy

¼ cup Italian or French dried mushrooms
1 cup hot water
1½ lbs. round steak (4 slices)
crushed garlic
3 tbsps. Parmesan cheese
½ tsp. parsley, chopped
2 tbsps. olive oil

2 tbsps. brandy
1 tbsp. flour
½ cup red wine
piece bay leaf (size of dime)
pinch basil
pinch oregano
salt and pepper
1 tbsp. tomato paste

Wash mushrooms and soak in hot water for an hour. Have butcher cut meat in thin slices and pound to make slices thinner. (See page 11.) Cut each slice in half, making 8 pieces. Put tiny dot of mixture of crushed garlic, 1 tsp. Parmesan cheese, and parsley in center of each slice, roll and tie with white string, at both ends. Brown quickly in hot oil in large skillet, rolling them back and forth as they brown. Flame with brandy and remove from pan.

To the pan add the mushrooms and water in which they are soaking, flour, wine, seasonings and tomato paste. Add the beef rolls, cover and cook for an hour or until tender. Serve in deep platter with bowl of Parmesan cheese on the side. Serves 4.

Braised Beef with Red Wine

Wine and spirit used:
  Brandy, red wine

Accompaniment:
  Bordeaux rouge or claret

1½ lbs. lean beef (round or sirloin)
2 tbsps. flour
3 tbsps. butter
2 tbsps. brandy
½ cup chopped onions
½ cup chopped celery
½ cup chopped carrots

½ cup chopped green peppers
1 large clove garlic, pressed
½ cup red wine
½ cup beef stock
salt and pepper
pinch oregano
chopped parsley or chives

Cut beef into 2-inch squares, roll in flour and brown quickly in large skillet in 2 tbsps. butter. Flame with brandy and remove from pan.
To the pan add the remaining tbsp. butter, all the vegetables, wine and stock. Return meat to the pan and add salt, pepper and oregano. Cover and cook on top of the stove until tender (approximately 1 hour).
To serve: Put the meat and vegetables in deep platter and sprinkle with fresh, chopped parsley or chives. Serves 4.

NOTE: *This dish can be cooked in a casserole in a 350° oven for about 2 hours instead of on top of the stove.*

Braised Leg of Lamb Bordeaux

Wine and spirit used:
  Brandy and sherry

Accompaniment:
  Beaujolais or Pinot Noir

½ leg of lamb (about 3 lbs.)
1 tbsp. butter or oil
3 tbsps. brandy
3 tbsps. sherry
pinch rosemary
pinch basil

1 medium onion, sliced
1 large clove garlic, pressed
1 tbsp. mint jelly
4 mushrooms, sliced
pinch oregano
salt and pepper

Cut fat from lamb and brown on all sides in heavy 5-quart

pot, in hot butter or oil over high heat. When brown, add rest of ingredients one by one. Cover tightly and cook over a very low flame until tender (approximately 1 hour). Serve on large platter and slice at table. Serve sauce separately. Serves 4.

California Pepper Steak

Wine used:
   Dry red wine

Accompaniment:
   White Côtes du Rhône or dry Semillon

2 green peppers
¼ cup plus 2 tbsps. olive oil
¼ lb. fresh mushrooms
3 fresh tomatoes
salt and pepper
pinch Ac'cent
pinch sugar
pinch oregano
1 lb. sirloin steak
¼ cup dry white wine

Cut the peppers in eighths, remove seeds and sauté pieces in ¼ cup oil until they are almost tender. Add the sliced mushrooms, toss a minute, add the tomatoes cut in eighths and seasonings. Remove from fire.

In another skillet heat 2 tbsps. oil, add steak cut in pieces or strips, and toss over high heat for five minutes. When ready to serve, put steak in same pan with the vegetables, add wine, heat and serve with noodles or mashed potatoes. Serves 4.

Chili con Carne y Frijoles

Wine used:
  Red wine

Accompaniment:
  Pinot Noir or Bordeaux rouge

- 1 lb. round steak
- 2 tbsps. oil
- 1 large onion, sliced
- 1 clove garlic, pressed
- ¼ tsp. cumin seeds
- salt and pepper
- pinch Ac'cent
- 1 green pepper, chopped
- 1 cup tomato sauce
- 1 tsp.-1 tbsp. chili powder (according to taste)
- ¼ cup red wine
- 1 can red kidney beans

Have steak cut in very thin strips. Brown by tossing quickly in hot oil over high flame. Remove from pan.

To the pan add onion first and then the rest of the ingredients, except the beans, and cook slowly until vegetables are tender. Put meat back in pan, add kidney beans and juice, cover and cook over low heat until meat is tender (approximately 45 minutes).

Serve with cornmeal mush or plain boiled rice in separate dishes. Serves 4.

Côtelette de Veau

Wines used:
  Sherry and white wine

Accompaniment:
  Bordeaux or Burgundy

- 2 thin veal cutlets (approximately 1½ lbs.)
- 1 tbsp. butter
- 2 tbsps. sherry
- 4 fresh mushrooms, finely sliced
- ½ tsp. tomato paste
- 1 tbsp. potato starch
- 1 cup beef stock
- 1 tbsp. red currant jelly
- ¼ cup white wine
- salt and white pepper

Pound cutlet thin, and separate the pieces where the membrane ends. Brown quickly in butter in large skillet. Flame with sherry and remove from pan.

To the pan add the mushrooms, tomato paste, potato starch, beef stock, jelly, wine, salt and pepper.

Mix well, return veal to pan, cover and cook slowly until tender (approximately 30-40 minutes).

To serve: Lay pieces of veal overlapping on hot serving platter, sprinkle with a little Parmesan cheese or chopped parsley and serve. Serves 4.

This is the French version of Veal Scallopini. Bon appétit!

Lamb Steaks à la Mode

Wine used:
  White wine

Accompaniment:
  Bernkastler or white Chianti

4 shoulder lamb steaks
  (round bone chops)
½ cup white wine
½ cup chili sauce

piece bay leaf (size of dime)
¼ tsp. dried basil
¼ tsp. dried tarragon
salt and pepper

Preheat oven to 350°. Put lamb chops, or steaks, in a long, flat dish suitable for marinating. Make marinade by combining all other ingredients, pour over steaks and keep in refrigerator for a day or two. When ready to cook, put steaks and sauce in baking dish and bake for 1 hour, basting occasionally. Serves 4.

NOTE: *These lamb steaks are often called "shoulder lamb chops." Be sure that they are all solid meat (except round bone) and that they are oval in shape and the kind that come 4 to an animal.*

Ossobuco Piemontese

Wine used:
: Italian white wine

Accompaniment:
: Soave or Orvieto

- 3 veal shanks, cut in 2" pieces
- 3 tbsps. olive oil
- 1 large onion, chopped
- 1 carrot, chopped
- 1 stalk celery, chopped
- 2 cloves garlic, crushed
- ¼ tsp. basil
- ¼ tsp. sage
- ¼ tsp. rosemary
- salt and white pepper
- 1 cup white wine
- ½ cup chicken stock
- ¼ cup tomato sauce

Dredge veal shanks in flour and brown quickly in hot oil, tossing them as they brown. Remove shanks to platter and prepare sauce. To the pan, add the onion, carrot, and celery and then the rest of the ingredients. Mix well, put meat back in pan, cover and cook until tender (approximately 1¼ hours). Serves 4.

Delicious served with fried eggplant and a salad.

Paupiettes de Veau aux Truffes
(Rolled Veal with Truffles)

Wine and spirit used:
  White wine and Cognac

Accompaniment:
  Graves or Pinot Blanc

- 2 thin veal cutlets (approximately 1½ lbs.)
- bread stuffing*
- 2 tbsps. butter or oil
- 2 tbsps. Cognac
- ¼ lb. fresh mushrooms, sliced
- 1 tbsp. flour
- 1 cup light stock
- 1 tbsp. tomato paste
- salt and pepper
- ¼ cup white wine
- 2 slices truffles or 1 tbsp. truffle purée
- chopped parsley

Cut the veal in 8 pieces, separating it along the membrane, and pound thin. Put 1 tbsp. bread stuffing on each piece of veal, roll and fasten with wooden toothpicks—or tie each end with piece of string.

Brown rolls (*paupiettes*) in butter or oil over high flame. Flame with Cognac and when flames die down, remove from pan. To the pan add the mushrooms, flour, stock, tomato paste, salt, pepper, and wine. Stir until smooth. Replace the *paupiettes*, cover and cook until tender (approximately 45 minutes).

To serve: Arrange *paupiettes* on platter, add truffles to sauce, pour sauce over meat and sprinkle with chopped parsley. Serves 4.

* *Bread Stuffing:* Sauté ½ onion, chopped, and ½ stalk celery, chopped, in 1 tbsp. butter until tender. Add salt, pepper, pinch thyme, pinch sage and two slices of white bread soaked in water and squeezed dry.

Saddle of Venison with Bourbon

Spirit used: Accompaniment:
  Bourbon   Burgundy

½ cup bourbon   6 whole cloves
1 onion, sliced   1 5-lb. saddle of venison
1 carrot, cut in 8ths   1 10-oz. jar of red currant jelly
6 peppercorns   ¼ tsp. salt

Preheat oven to 350°. Combine the bourbon, onion, carrot and seasonings in a deep bowl. Add the venison and leave in marinade for 2 hours, turning every 15 minutes.

Remove meat, place in roasting pan, and make sauce by melting the jelly in a 1-quart pan over direct flame, adding the marinade and cooking a minute or two until smooth. Bake venison for 2-2½ hours, basting with the sauce every 15 minutes, until the meat takes on a shiny glaze. (If any sauce remains, it may be served on the side with the sliced meat.) Serves 6.

Venison may also be cut into steaks and broiled. Baste on both sides with same sauce as above, to give a glossy finish.

Saltimbocca

Spirit used: Accompaniment:
  Brandy   Bardolino or California red wine

1½ lbs. (8 pieces) veal   ¼ lb. prosciutto
  scallops   2 tbsps. olive oil
salt and white pepper   2 tbsps. brandy
pinch basil   ¼ cup chicken stock
pinch sage   ¼ cup Cognac

Sprinkle scallops with basil, salt, pepper and sage. (It is the sage that identifies the dish.) Cut slices of prosciutto to same size as scallops and fasten slices and scallops together in pairs with wooden toothpicks, by weaving a toothpick through each pair. Brown quickly in oil over high heat, tossing as they brown. Flame with brandy and transfer to a serving platter. To juices in pan add the chicken stock, heat and pour over meat.

This is another good company dish, to be kept hot in a chafing dish. It may also be served as an appetizer, by cutting into bite-size pieces and serving on toast points.

Sauerbraten

Spirit used:
  Beer

Accompaniment:
  Beer

4-lb. chuck roast
1 large bay leaf
½ tsp. black peppercorns
1 cup dark brown sugar
1 can beer

¼ tsp. ground cloves
3 carrots
3 onions
12 ginger snaps
salt and pepper

Wipe meat with a damp paper towel. Put in deep glass, glazed, enamel or stainless steel pot, mix together all other ingredients except ginger snaps and pour over. Cover tightly and marinate for 1 week (if possible), turning each day with a wooden fork or spoon. When ready to bake, put in deep cooking pot, add some of the marinade and cook, covered, for 2 to 3 hours over low heat. When meat is tender, remove from pot, add ginger snaps to thicken the gravy and pour over meat. Serves 8.

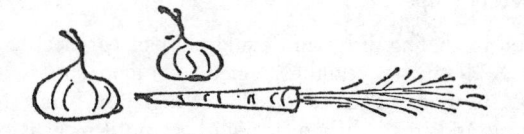

Steak Diane

Wine and spirit used:
  Dry vermouth and Cognac

Accompaniment:
  Burgundy

4 filets of sirloin steak
salt and pepper
2 tbsps. butter
¼ cup Cognac

½ cup dry vermouth
2 tbsps. Worcestershire Sauce
1 tbsp. finely chopped chives

Have the steaks pounded very thin, but do *not* let the butcher put them through a tenderizing machine. Season them with salt and pepper. Melt butter in the crêpe pan of chafing dish, or in any shallow 12-inch pan, and when hot, add steaks. Cook for 2 minutes on each side. Flame with Cognac, add the vermouth, Worcestershire and chives and stir. Pour juices over steak and serve. Serves 4.

Sukiyaki

Wine used:
  Saki

Accompaniment:
  Saki

3 tbsps. peanut oil
2 onions, coarsely chopped
1 bunch scallions, cut in 1-inch pieces
3 stalks celery, cut diagonally in 1-inch pieces
1 cup canned bamboo shoots, sliced in strips

¼ lb. fresh mushrooms, sliced
1 tbsp. sugar
¼ cup soy sauce
¼ cup saki
1-lb. sirloin steak, cut paper thin in strips

Pour oil in chafing dish pan or sukiyaki pan (or electric frying pan). Add onions, scallions, celery, bamboo shoots, mushrooms, sugar, soy sauce and saki. When just barely tender, add meat and toss lightly over high heat until meat is cooked to your liking. Add more saki, if too dry.

American or imported Riesling may be substituted, if saki is unobtainable.

This famous Japanese dish may also be made with spinach and thin slices of raw chicken instead of steak.

Sweetbreads d'Anjou

Wine and spirit used:
  Brandy and sherry

Accompaniment:
  Beaujolais or Burgundy

- 1 pair of sweetbreads (*approximately* 1½ *lbs.*)
- 1 tbsp. lemon juice
- 1 tsp. salt
- 5 tbsps. flour
- 4 tbsps. butter
- 2 tbsps. brandy
- ½ lb. fresh mushrooms, sliced
- salt and pepper
- ½ tsp. paprika
- 1 cup milk
- ¼ cup sherry
- 1 pimento, chopped

Soak sweetbreads for 30 minutes in cold water to which the lemon juice and 1 tsp. salt have been added. Remove and pat dry with paper towels. Dry further by rolling them in 2 tbsps. flour which has been spread on waxed paper. Remove any tubes or membranes and cut in bite-sized pieces with kitchen shears.

Melt 1 tbsp. butter in large skillet and when hot, sauté sweetbreads quickly until brown on all sides. Flame with brandy and remove from pan. Add the mushrooms to the pan and sauté, tossing them in order to absorb any butter remaining in the pan. Remove and place with sweetbreads.

Sauce: Melt remaining 3 tbsps. butter and away from the flame add flour, salt, pepper, paprika, milk, and sherry. Stir, put back on the fire and cook, while stirring, until sauce thickens. Add sweetbreads and mushrooms and stir until they are combined with the sauce. (More cooking would toughen the sweetbreads.) Add the pimento, arrange on toast points or in puff-paste shells and sprinkle with chopped parsley. Serves 4.

Veal Scallopini alla Romano

Wine used:
Sherry and Marsala

Accompaniment:
Verdicchi or white Chianti

2 thin veal cutlets
 (*approximately 1½ lbs.*)
½ *cup flour*
pinch cayenne pepper
pinch nutmeg
pinch dry mustard
pinch basil

salt and pepper
¼ *tsp. sugar*
2 *tbsps. olive oil*
2 *tbsps. sherry*
5 *mushrooms, sliced*
½ *cup Marsala*
juice of ½ lemon (1 tbsp.)

chopped parsley

Pound cutlet thin and separate pieces where the membrane ends. Put flour and all the seasonings on piece of waxed paper and mix well with your fingers. Coat veal pieces with flour mixture and pat well so that not much flour remains on them. Brown quickly over high heat in oil, flame with sherry and remove from pan.

To the pan add the mushrooms, Marsala and lemon juice, stir until sauce thickens and pour immediately over veal pieces. Sprinkle with chopped parsley and serve. Serves 4.

Italian work of art fit for the Uffizi.

Vegetables

Baked Vegetables Brazilian

Wine used:
  Red wine

Accompaniment:
  Pinot Noir or Brazilian red wine

- 1 pkg. frozen chopped spinach
- 2 green peppers, seeded and chopped
- 1 medium onion, chopped
- 2 tbsps. black raisins
- ½ tsp. salt
- pinch allspice
- 1 tsp. cumin seed
- ¼ tsp. chili powder
- ½ cup tomato juice
- ¼ cup red wine
- ¼ cup dry bread crumbs
- ½ cup grated Parmesan cheese
- 1 tbsp. butter

Preheat oven to 400°. Defrost spinach and drain. In a 1-quart casserole combine spinach, peppers, onion, raisins, seasonings, tomato juice, and wine. Sprinkle with bread crumbs and cheese, dot with butter and bake for 1 hour. Serves 6.

Burgundy Onions

Wine used:
  Burgundy

- 4 Bermuda onions
- ¾ cup Burgundy
- 1 tbsp. sugar
- salt and white pepper

Slice onions paper thin. Pour Burgundy into a large 10-inch skillet, add onions, sugar, salt and white pepper. Cover and cook until onions are tender and have taken on the color of the wine. A tbsp. butter may be added just before serving to give the onions a shine. Serve hot or cold. Serves 6.

Excellent with cold roast beef, pheasant or turkey.

Cauliflower Loaf

Wine used:
Dry sherry

1 tbsp. butter
2 pkgs. frozen cauliflower
1 cup Béchamel sauce
3 eggs
salt and pepper
2 tbsps. dry sherry
paprika
pinch caraway seeds or dill seeds
Mornay sauce

Preheat oven to 375°. Melt butter in 10" skillet, add frozen cauliflower. (Do not defrost.) Cover pan and cook over low heat until tender (approximately 6 minutes). Puree in blender or run through a coarse strainer. Combine with Béchamel sauce, add eggs, salt and pepper to taste, sherry, and caraway seeds—or dill seeds, if desired. Sprinkle with paprika and bake for 30 to 35 minutes. Unmold loaf on deep platter and cover with Mornay sauce. Serves 6-8.

Duchesse Potatoes

4 or 5 white potatoes
2 tbsps. butter
2 tbsps. milk
1 whole egg
pinch salt

Peel potatoes and cook until soft in just enough water to cover them. Drain, add butter, milk, egg and salt, beating after each addition. Put mixture in pastry bag with a #5 star tube and pipe onto heat-proof platter. Using pastry brush, brush on egg wash (1 egg yolk plus 1 tbsp. water, beaten with fork).

(See Lobster Cordon Bleu)

Glazed Carrots Supreme

Spirit used:
  Orange liqueur

1 bunch slender fresh carrots   ¼ cup orange liqueur*
2 tbsps. butter   few grains of salt

Wash and brush carrots to clean them well. In an 8-inch flat skillet, melt the butter, add the carrots and water that clings to them, then the liqueur. Salt lightly. Cover and let simmer on a very low heat till tender (approximately 15 minutes), turning to be sure all sides are coated. Serves 4.

*Two tablespoons of light brown sugar may be substituted for orange liqueur.

A colorful side dish for meat, fish or fowl and a delightful change from the usual combination of carrots and peas.

Onions Aleatico

Wine used:
  Aleatico*

12 medium onions   ¼ cup Aleatico
¾ cup heavy cream   1 tbsp. butter
         salt and white pepper

Preheat oven to 350°. Slice onions and boil in water to cover until tender (approximately 10 minutes). Drain and put in greased baking dish 9″ x 6″ x 2″. Add cream, wine, salt and pepper. Dot with butter and bake for 30 minutes. Serves 8.

* *Italian Muscatel.*

Red Cabbage with Wine

Wine used:
  Red wine

- 2 tbsps. butter
- 1 small onion, minced
- 1 medium head red cabbage (2 lbs.)
- 1 green apple, peeled and grated
- ½ cup red wine
- ½ cup red currant jelly
- pinch salt
- 1 tbsp. flour

Melt butter in deep 3-quart pan. Sauté the onion until golden, then add cabbage, shredded coarsely, apple, red wine, jelly and salt. Cover and cook over low heat until tender. Remove from fire, sprinkle on flour, and return to fire. Heat and stir until mixture has thickened a bit. Cover and keep hot until ready to serve. Serves 6.

An excellent accompaniment for pork or fowl. If red cabbage is not available, use white.

Sweet Potato Puffs

Spirit used:
  Orange liqueur

2 lbs. sweet potatoes	⅓ cup milk
2 tbsps. butter	¼ cup orange liqueur
½ tsp. salt	⅓ cup orange marmalade
8 orange cups*	

Preheat oven to 350°. Boil sweet potatoes, cool, remove jackets and mash them well. Add butter, salt, milk, and orange liqueur. Fill the scooped-out orange shells, spread top with marmalade and bake for 30 minutes. Serves 8.

Orange cups (rinds of halves of oranges) may be saved up by keeping them in a plastic bag in refrigerator until ready to use.

Breads

Banana Bread

Spirit used:
  Beer

⅓ cup butter
¾ cup sugar
2 eggs
1 cup mashed bananas
1¾ cups flour

¾ tsp. salt
1¼ tsps. baking powder
½ tsp. baking soda
¼ cup beer
½ cup chopped walnuts

Preheat oven to 350°. Cream the butter and sugar, add the eggs one at a time, walnuts, and then the mashed bananas alternately with the flour. Add salt, baking powder and soda and then the beer. Grease a bread pan with butter, pour in mixture and bake for 55 minutes. Makes 1 loaf.

Beer Bread

Spirit used:
  Beer

1 cup beer
1 pkg. dry yeast
4 tbsps. melted butter
½ cup light brown sugar

2 cups all-purpose flour
1 cup whole wheat flour
½ cup wheat germ
½ tsp. salt

Preheat oven to 375°. Heat beer to lukewarm in a 1-quart pan. Remove from fire and sprinkle on the dry yeast. Add pinch of sugar to start the fermentation and set pan aside until mixture bubbles. In a large 4-quart bowl, place 2 tbsps. of the melted butter, sugar, flours, wheat germ and salt. Add beer and yeast mixture. Stir quickly to incorporate the ingredients. Turn out on a working area and knead a minute or two. Grease bowl with 1 tbsp. of the melted butter, return dough to bowl and let rise until double in bulk (about 1 hour). When risen, turn out again on working area and knead another minute. Shape into a loaf and place in greased bread pan, approximately 8 x 4 x 2½ inches. Brush top of loaf with butter and let rise again until it reaches the top of the pan. Bake for about one hour or until the top of the loaf is crisp and brown. Makes one loaf.

Christmas Panetone

Wine used:
Marsala

- 2 pkgs. dry yeast
- 1 cup lukewarm water
- ½ cup sugar
- ¼ lb. butter (1 strip)
- 2 tsps. salt
- 3 eggs
- 3 egg yolks
- ¼ cup Marsala
- 5½ cups sifted all-purpose flour
- ½ cup citron, chopped
- 1 cup seedless raisins
- ½ cup glazed fruits, chopped

Preheat oven to 450°. Soften yeast in warm water, sprinkle ¼ tsp. sugar over to start fermentation. In a very large bowl, mix butter, salt, sugar, whole eggs, 2 egg yolks and Marsala. Then add yeast mixture and flour. Stir until ingredients are blended. Turn out on a floured working area and knead until dough is smooth and free from stickiness. Knead in the citron, raisins and fruits. Place in large bowl, which has been greased with 1 tbsp. butter and let rise until double in bulk (approximately 2 hours). Remove dough from bowl, divide into two parts, knead into shape and place each in a 1-quart greased soufflé dish or straight-sided 1-quart dish. With kitchen shears cut a deep cross on the top of the loaf and brush on egg wash (1 egg yolk plus 1 tbsp. water) to make the loaf shiny.

Bake for 5 minutes then reduce heat to 350° and bake for 25 to 30 minutes more. Makes two loaves.

Jamaican Date and Nut Bread

Spirit used:
  Rum

1 8-oz. pkg. dates	1 cup dark brown sugar
1 cup walnuts, chopped	pinch of salt
2 tsps. baking soda	3 cups all-purpose flour, sifted
2 eggs	¼ cup Jamaica rum
2 tbsps. melted butter	

Preheat oven to 350°. Cut dates in pieces and put in bowl with walnuts and baking soda. Pour 1½ cups boiling water over and let cool. Separate eggs and put yolks in large bowl of electric mixer. Add sugar, start mixer, then add date mixture alternately with flour, salt and rum. Fold in stiffly beaten egg whites and melted butter. Pour mixture into two greased loaf pans and bake for 45 to 60 minutes.

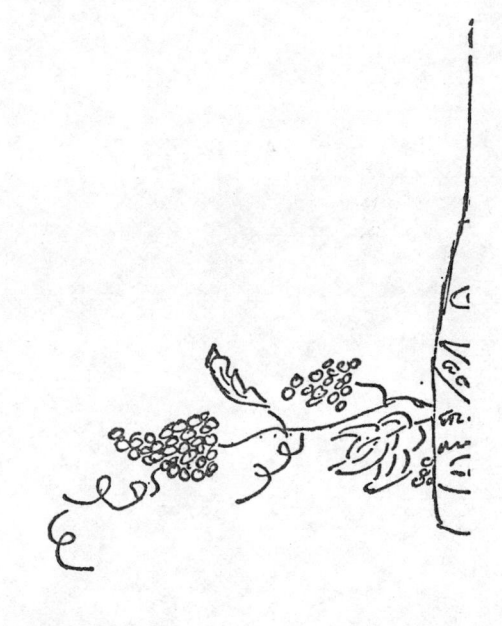

Sauces

Barbecue Sauce

Wine used:
  Red wine

Accompaniment:
  Cabernet Sauvignon or Pinot Noir

1 tbsp. butter
1 small onion, chopped
2 tbsps. dark brown sugar
2 tbsps. prepared mustard
½ cup red wine
1 tbsp. Worcestershire sauce
1 cup catsup
½ cup water
1 cup tomato sauce

Melt butter in 1-quart pan, add chopped onion and cook until it is soft (approximately 5 minutes). Add rest of ingredients and cook for 5 minutes more over a low flame. May be stored in refrigerator in pint-size jar with a screw-on cover until needed.

Béarnaise Sauce

Wine used:
  Dry white wine (Chablis or Pinot)

3 egg yolks
2 tbsps. dry white wine
1 tbsp. tarragon vinegar
½ tsp. lemon juice
pinch cayenne pepper
2 tbsps. heavy cream
3 tbsps. butter
½ tsp. meat glacé*
1 tbsp. chopped parsley
6 capers

Put egg yolks and wine in a 6-inch earthenware bowl over water or in the top of a double boiler. Mix with wire whisk. Add vinegar, lemon juice, pepper and cream. Cook and stir over simmering water until sauce begins to thicken. Add butter, meat glacé, parsley and capers and cook until thick. Serve warm—not hot. Makes 1 cup sauce.

* *Concentrated meat stock.*

Béchamel Sauce (White Sauce)

1 cup milk	piece bay leaf (size of dime)
1 small onion sliced	salt and white pepper
or pinch onion powder	2 tbsps. butter
½ carrot	2 tbsps. flour
1 stalk celery	
or pinch celery powder	

Bring milk and vegetables to a boil in a 1-quart pan. Add bay leaf, salt and pepper and simmer a minute. Strain. In another pan of the same size, melt the butter and add flour away from the fire. Stir until smooth and gradually add the flavored milk. Put pan back on fire and gently stir until it just comes to a boil.

Béchamel sauce by itself is a good sauce for vegetables, fish or fowl and is also used as the base for more elaborate French sauces.

Bigarade Sauce for Roast Duck and Game Birds

Wine and spirit used:
   Sherry and orange liqueur

1 cup sherry	1 tbsp. tomato paste
2 tbsps. orange liqueur	1 cup chicken stock
1 tbsp. red currant jelly	1 tbsp. potato starch
1 orange	

Squeeze orange and cut rind into fine julienne strips. Put sherry and liqueur in a 1-quart pot, then add jelly, tomato paste, chicken stock and potato starch. Bring to a boil and beat very well with a wire whisk. Add the finely sliced rind of orange and the juice (½ cup). Toss until the rind is coated with the sauce and pour over the roasted duck. Flame and serve.

This famous French sauce takes its name from the Bigarade or bitter orange, known also as the Seville orange.

Bordelaise Sauce for Steak or Roasts

Wine used:
Red Bordeaux

1 shallot or tiny onion, chopped	½ cup Red Bordeaux
pinch pepper	½ cup of strong beef stock
pinch salt	1 tbsp. butter
pinch marjoram	1 tbsp. parsley, chopped
pinch thyme	marrow from marrow bone (optional)
piece of bay leaf (size of dime)	

Combine shallot or onion, pepper, salt, marjoram, thyme and bay leaf with wine. Simmer until wine is reduced by half, add beef stock and reduce the sauce again to one half. Add butter and parsley. (Marrow from the marrow bone may be added if desired, but it is not necessary.) Makes ½ cup.

Cumberland Sauce for Game

Wine used:
Ruby port

¾ cup red currant jelly	1 tbsp. prepared mustard
¼ cup ruby port	1 tsp. paprika
⅓ cup orange juice	½ tsp. ground ginger
1 tbsp. lemon juice	3 tbsps. shredded orange rind

Melt jelly over low heat in a 1-quart pan until it liquefies. Cool and add wine, juices, and spices. Put back on stove, add orange rind, cook for a minute to incorporate flavors and serve.

Hollandaise Sauce

3 egg yolks	1 tbsp. lemon juice
1 tsp. tarragon vinegar	3 tbsps. butter
2 tbsps. cream or milk	

In the top of a double boiler, place egg yolks, vinegar, and lemon juice. Cook over hot, but not boiling, water until it thickens, stirring constantly with a wire whisk. Add cream (or milk) and butter, continuing to beat with wire whisk.

This is a fool-proof Hollandaise sauce. It will not curdle and can stand for as long as an hour before serving. If it thickens, add more cream or milk to thin it and beat with a wire whisk.

Mornay Sauce

2 tbsps. butter	¼ cup finely grated Swiss cheese
2 tbsps. flour	
1 cup chicken stock	¼ cup finely grated Parmesan cheese
salt and white pepper	
½ cup milk	¼ cup light cream (optional)

Melt butter in 1-quart pan. Take off fire and blend in flour, then chicken stock, milk, salt and pepper. Cook, stirring constantly, until thick and smooth. Add grated cheeses and when they are melted, stir in the cream.

Weight-watchers may omit the cream.

Sauce Dijon for Steaks

Wines and spirit used:
  Brandy, sherry and Madeira

½ lb. fresh mushrooms, sliced	salt and pepper
4 tbsps. butter	2 tbsps. brandy
1 tsp. flour	1 tbsp. sherry
	1 tbsp. Madeira
1 tbsp. Dijon mustard*	

Wash and slice mushrooms, reserving stems for another dish. Sauté in 2 tbsps. butter for 5 minutes. Sprinkle flour over, add salt and pepper and mix. Warm the brandy, sherry and Madeira in a small pan, set aflame and pour over mushrooms. Then add remaining butter and the mustard. Stir for a minute until sauce thickens slightly. Pour immediately over slices of broiled steak.

*Dijon mustard has a white wine base.

Spaghetti Sauce alla Piemontese

Wine used:
    Italian red wine

Accompaniment:
    Fine red Chianti

2 tbsps. dried Italian
    mushrooms
1 cup boiling water
1 lb. veal (rump or shoulder)
2 tbsps. olive oil
4 large onions

1 cup tomato sauce
½ cup red wine
½ tsp. basil
1 large clove garlic, crushed
salt and pepper
1 tsp. meat glacé

Wash mushrooms and soak in boiling water for an hour to soften them. Brown veal in olive oil in a 3-quart pot. Add onions, tomato sauce (reserving 2 tbsps. for later use), wine, seasonings and meat glacé, mushrooms and water in which they are soaking. Cover and cook until meat is tender (approximately 1 hour). Remove meat from sauce and grind it, using coarse ring of grinder. Return meat to sauce and stir until it is well mixed. Add rest of tomato sauce to give a bright red color. Correct seasonings and serve over spaghetti or fancy-shaped pasta. Can be made in advance as flavor improves in the keeping. Serves 4.

A famous dish of the Piedmont district of Italy.

Miscellaneous

Flaky Pie Crust

1½ cups all-purpose flour
pinch salt
¼ cup butter
¼ cup solid shortening
½ cup ice water

Preheat oven to 400°. Blend shortenings into flour and salt roughly, leaving large lumps (size of a nickel). It is better not to cut the shortening any finer. Gradually add ice water. Mix until flour absorbs water and dough pulls away from side of the bowl. Turn out on floured working area and roll to size of pie tin (divide in half before rolling for two-crust pie). Grease pie plate with 1 tbsp. butter. This recipe makes enough crust for a 9-inch two-crust pie or a 10- to 11-inch pie shell, 1½ inches deep. For a shell, put a 6" x 6" square of waxed paper over crust before baking and ½ cup rice or dried beans over that. Bake for 25 minutes, removing rice or beans and waxed paper after the first 15 minutes. Bake until lightly golden.

Fruit Stuffing for Fowl

1 tbsp. butter
1 small onion, chopped
½ cup diced celery
½ cup dry bread crumbs
1 cup cooked rice
pinch salt, marjoram, sage, thyme and white pepper
½ cup pineapple tidbits
½ cup orange pieces
¼ cup raisins
2 tbsps. blanched, slivered almonds

Melt butter, add onions and celery and cook until tender. Add bread crumbs, rice, seasoning, fruits and almonds. Stuff fowl loosely. Makes 2 cups.

See recipe for Cornish Hen Plymouth.

Hawaiian Salad Dressing

Spirit used:
  Pineapple or banana liqueur

½ cup salad oil
½ cup pineapple juice
1 tsp. lemon juice
pinch salt

1 ripe banana
2 tbsps. pineapple or banana liqueur

Put oil, juices, salt and banana in blender. Blend for 1 minute and add liqueur. Blend again until thick and smooth. If you do not have a blender, add other ingredients and beat. Makes 1¼ cups dressing.

Honey-Orange Dressing for Fruit Salad

Spirit used:
  Orange liqueur

1 3-oz. pkg. cream cheese
1 tbsp. honey

¼ cup orange liqueur
1 orange

Squeeze orange and grate rind. Put cream cheese and honey in 1-quart bowl and work in juice and rind of orange. Add liqueur and blend well. Makes 1 cup salad dressing. May be kept in a jar and used as needed.

Jellied Cucumber Salad

Wine used:
 White wine

2 tbsps. gelatin	1 tsp. salt
¼ cup cold water	¼ cup cider vinegar
¼ cup white wine	juice of 2 lemons (6 tbsps.)
1½ cups boiling water	2 medium cucumbers,
½ cup sugar	coarsely grated

Soak gelatin in cold water and wine in 2-quart bowl for 5 minutes or until it is softened. Add boiling water and stir. Add sugar, salt, vinegar and lemon juice and set bowl in refrigerator until mixture thickens a bit.

Grate the cucumbers (skin on) with a coarse grater and add to the slightly thickened gelatin mixture. Pour into 1-quart mold that has been greased with corn oil and place in refrigerator to harden. Serves 8 to 10.

An excellent buffet dish especially when a combination of fish, fowl or meat is served, as it goes with all three. Shredded cabbage can be substituted for cucumbers.

Swedish Avocado

Wine used:
 Madeira or port

¼ lb. fresh mushrooms	1 avocado
3 tbsps. butter	¼ cup Madeira or port
3 tbsps. flour	pinch salt
½ cup milk	pinch paprika

Slice mushrooms and sauté them in butter for two minutes. Remove mushrooms and add flour to the pan away from flame. Add milk, stir until smooth and cook until thick. Peel avocado, remove stone and cut in thin slices. Add avocado slices, sautéed mushrooms, Madeira or port and seasoning and mix lightly. Serves 4.

Goes beautifully with fish or fowl.

Wild Rice

Wine used:
  Sherry or Madeira

| 1 cup wild rice | pinch salt |
| 2 cups chicken stock | 1 tbsp. butter |

¼ cup sherry or Madeira

Place rice in a colander and let tap water run through until it becomes clear. Put rice in a deep 3-quart pot with just enough water to cover and let soak overnight. When ready to cook, drain, add chicken stock and cook over low heat without cover until tender (approximately 20 minutes). Add salt and butter and toss rice until it is shiny. Add the sherry or Madeira, cover and set aside until ready to serve. May be reheated directly over low heat.

This dish is an excellent accompaniment for game, fowl or fish, and may be frozen for future use. Vary it by adding ¼ cup dark raisins and ¼ cup sliced, blanched almonds.

Cakes and Cookies

Apricot Bars

Spirit used:
 Apricot liqueur

1 cup dried apricots	1 cup light brown sugar
½ cup butter	¼ cup apricot liqueur
¼ cup white sugar	½ cup walnuts, chopped
1⅓ cups flour	¼ tsp. salt
2 eggs	½ tsp. baking powder

Preheat oven to 350°. Rinse apricots, add 1 cup water, and boil uncovered in a 1-quart saucepan for 10 minutes or until tender and water is evaporated. When cool, cut in small pieces with kitchen shears and leave in pan. In a small bowl combine butter, sugar and 1 cup flour and pack mixture, pressing down with fingers, in the bottom of a greased square pan 9" x 9" x 2". Bake this layer for 15 minutes. While it is baking, beat eggs with light brown sugar and add liqueur, ⅓ cup flour, apricots, nuts, salt and baking powder. When first layer is baked, remove from oven, spread with apricot mixture and bake for 30 minutes more. Cool and cut into squares or bars, sprinkle with confectioner's sugar and store in a covered tin. Makes 36 squares or 48 bars.

These bars freeze very well and can be packed for mailing.

Baba au Rhum—New Orleans Style

Spirit used:
  Light or dark rum

Cake:
6 eggs, separated
¾ cup sugar
1 tbsp. lemon rind (grated)
1 cup sifted flour
pinch salt
1 tsp. baking powder

Syrup:
½ cup sugar
1 can (12-oz.) apricot nectar
1 tbsp. lemon juice
¼ cup rum
1 cup whipped cream

Cake:
Mix egg yolks and sugar in large bowl and beat until they are light in color. Add lemon rind, flour and salt. Beat egg whites until very stiff and combine with yolk mixture. Add baking powder very carefully. Bake in tube pan in 350° oven for 45 minutes. Cool.

Syrup:
Boil sugar and apricot nectar together for 10 minutes. Add lemon juice and rum. Cool.

When both the cake and syrup are cool, put cake back in pan it was baked in and pour over syrup gradually. Leave cake in pan until you are ready to serve it. Fill center with whipped cream flavored with rum. Serves 8 to 10.

Individual babas may be baked in muffin tins.

Babka

Spirit used:
  Light rum

¼ cup milk
¼ cup water
1 pkg. dry yeast
¼ cup sugar
¼ cup butter
3 eggs
2½ cups flour
pinch salt
¼ cup candied fruits
¼ cup raisins

Preheat oven to 375°. Heat milk and water to lukewarm and sprinkle yeast over it. Add pinch of sugar to start fermentation and set aside until it bubbles. Combine butter, sugar, eggs, flour and salt in a large bowl. Add yeast mixture and let rise in a warm place until double in bulk (approximately 1 hour). Stir in the fruits and raisins and turn out on a working area and knead for about a minute. Place in a greased 2-quart mold or kuglegof pan and let rise again until doubled. Bake for 30-35 minutes. Remove from pan and while still hot, brush on rum glaze generously with pastry brush.

Rum Glaze: Combine ½ cup granulated sugar, 2 tbsps. rum and 2 tbsps. water in a small pan. Bring to a boil and boil briskly for one minute.

Coffee Bavarian Cream Cake

Spirit used:
  Coffee liqueur

4 eggs
3 tbsps. sugar
1 cup milk
1 tbsp. instant coffee
1 tbsp. gelatin
1 cup heavy cream, whipped
¼ cup coffee liqueur
1 layer sponge cake
1 square bitter chocolate

Separate the eggs. In a 1-quart pan place the egg yolks, sugar, milk, instant coffee and gelatin. Cook over low heat, stirring very well until mixture thickens, being careful not to let it boil. Cool custard quickly by putting it in a large bowl over ice cubes or in the refrigerator. When cool, add the stiffly beaten egg whites, whipped cream and liqueur.

Place an 8-inch sponge layer in an 8-inch spring form. Pour the cooled custard over the layer and place in refrigerator overnight to become firm and to mellow. When ready to serve, remove the sides of the spring form and sprinkle top with shaved chocolate.

To shave chocolate: Run potato peeler over squares of chocolate. Chocolate curls as it falls on the cake.

Chocolate Rum Chips

Spirit used:
  Jamaican rum

2 squares baking chocolate
½ cup butter (¼ lb.)
1 cup light brown sugar
1 egg
3 tbsps. milk
½ tsp. dried orange rind
1¾ cups all-purpose flour
3 tbsps. rum
1 pkg. chocolate chips or bits
1 tsp. baking powder

Preheat oven to 375°. Melt chocolate over hot water. Cream butter with sugar, add egg, milk, orange rind and then flour alternately with rum. Add melted chocolate and chips and lastly the baking powder. Drop by teaspoonfuls on a lightly greased cookie tin and bake for 15 minutes. Makes approximately 3 dozen.

Crowning Glory (Cream Puff Ring)

Spirit used:
Rum

1 cup water
¼ lb. butter
1 cup sifted flour
4 whole eggs

2 tbsps. slivered almonds
1 cup heavy cream, whipped
confectioner's sugar
rum chocolate filling

Put water and butter in a 1-quart pan and let come to a boil quickly. Remove pan from fire, add flour. Then beat in the eggs one at a time, beating after each egg is added to make a paste. Grease a cookie sheet with butter and with your finger draw a 9-inch circle. Put the paste in a pastry bag and pipe out the dough in a ring, using the circle as a guide. Overlap where the ends meet. Sprinkle top of dough with sliced, blanched almonds and bake in preheated 375° oven for 30 minutes. When baked, remove from oven and with a very sharp knife cut the circle in half horizontally. Take off the top half very carefully and set aside while you fill the bottom half. Pipe out rum chocolate filling over bottom half in alternate two-inch spaces. Fill in remaining spaces with whipped cream. Put on top half and sprinkle with confectioner's sugar.

Rum Chocolate Filling

½ cup cocoa
½ cup sugar
½ tsp. salt

¼ cup flour
1 cup milk
2 egg yolks

2 tbsps. rum

Mix cocoa, sugar, salt and flour in a small pan. Add milk and then egg yolks, beating with a wire whisk until all the ingredients are mixed. Place pan over low heat and cook until mixture thickens. Remove pan from fire and add rum. The filling must be very thick in order to keep its shape when it is piped out of the pastry bag.

A very beautiful and delicate dessert that is worth the extra time involved in making it. If desired, only one of the fillings can be used instead of both.

French Apricot Filling

Spirit used:
  Apricot liqueur*

2½ cups milk	½ tsp. salt
¾ cup sugar	¼ cup apricot liqueur*
½ cup flour	3 eggs
3 tbsps. butter	

Scald the milk in the top of a double boiler, by placing top directly on the fire and bringing to a boil. Add sugar, flour, salt and liqueur and cook over hot water, stirring with wire whisk, until it thickens. Remove from fire and add eggs. Cook 2 minutes more, beating well. Add butter, stir and chill until ready to fill pastry or a sponge roll.

* Any fruit liqueur may be substituted.

Fudge Rounds

Spirit used:
  Coffee liqueur

1 cup sugar	1½ cups uncooked oatmeal
¾ cup butter (1½ strips)	2 squares unsweetened chocolate
½ tsp. salt	
1½ cups flour	¼ cup chopped nuts or sugar sprinkles
¼ cup coffee liqueur	

Preheat oven to 375°. Blend sugar and butter thoroughly. Add salt, flour, liqueur, oats and melted chocolate. Shape the dough into a large ball. Pinch off pieces of dough and shape to size of nickel. Place on an ungreased cookie tin and sprinkle with nuts or sugar sprinkles. Bake for 12 minutes. Makes 3 dozen.

A delicious cookie that keeps well.

German Beer Cake

Spirit used:
  Dark beer

1 cup molasses
¼ cup butter or oil
2 eggs
1 cup dark beer
2½ cups all-purpose flour, sifted

1 cup dark, seedless raisins
½ tsp. ginger
¼ tsp. cinnamon
¼ tsp. cloves
¼ tsp. nutmeg
½ cup chopped walnuts

1½ tsps. baking soda

Preheat oven to 350°. In a large bowl mix the molasses and butter or oil. Add eggs and beat until well blended. Add beer alternately with flour and then the raisins, seasonings, nuts and lastly the baking soda. Bake in a greased 9" x 13" x 2" baking dish for 45-50 minutes. Remove from oven and sprinkle top with sesame seeds or, using sesame seeds, "draw" a beer stein on top of the cake.

A delicious and healthful cake that keeps for days.

Gin and Butter Wafers

Spirit used:
  Gin

½ lb. butter
¼ cup verifine sugar
1 egg yolk

2 tbsps. wheat germ
1 tbsp. gin
2 cups all-purpose flour

Preheat oven to 375°. Blend butter and sugar in electric mixer. Add egg yolk, wheat germ, gin and flour and mix at low speed until incorporated. Remove dough from bowl to a working area, divide in half and roll each half into a "salami-style" roll, sprinkling with a bit of flour to keep dough from sticking. Wrap each roll in waxed paper and store in refrigerator until stiff (at least 3 hours). The roll may be kept in the refrigerator for a week or may be frozen. When ready to bake, cut in slices the thickness of a half dollar, place on cookie tin and bake in a preheated 375° oven for 12 minutes or until light brown. Makes about 5 dozen.
Optional: Beat egg white slightly and brush each cookie. Sprinkle with nuts or sesame seeds or decorate with green and red candied cherries cut in shapes.

The piquant taste of juniper berries in the gin imparts an unusual flavor to these cookies.

Gingerbread

Spirit used:
  Rum

½ cup butter
½ cup sugar
1 egg
2½ cups all-purpose flour
1½ tsps. baking soda
½ tsp. salt

1 cup molasses
¾ cup hot water
¼ cup rum
¼ tsp. cinnamon
1 tsp. powdered ginger
½ tsp. powdered cloves

whipped cream

Preheat oven to 350°. Put butter in a large bowl, add the sugar and then the egg and beat well. Sift flour with soda and salt and add to first mixture alternately with molasses, water and rum. Add spices, pour into greased 9" x 12" x 2" pan and bake for 45 minutes. Remove from pan, cool, and top with whipped cream.

Happy Apple Cake

Spirit used:
  Whiskey

¼ cup melted butter
1 cup light brown sugar
3 or 4 tart apples, sliced
3 eggs, separated

1 cup granulated sugar
¼ cup whiskey
1 cup all-purpose flour
1 tsp. baking powder

whipped cream

Preheat oven to 350°. Melt the butter and pour into a 9" x 9" x 2" square pan. Spread the sugar over the butter and cover with apple slices. Put egg yolks in large bowl, add granulated sugar and mix well for 5 minutes. Add the whiskey and then the flour and baking powder, which have been sifted together. Beat the egg whites until stiff and fold in well. Pour this mixture over the apples and bake for 45-50 minutes. Turn out, while hot, onto platter and serve in separate portions with a dab of whiskey-flavored whipped cream on top. Serves 8 to 10.

Orange Tipple Cake

Spirit used:
  Orange liqueur

½ cup butter or oil	¼ cup orange liqueur
1 cup sugar	2 cups all-purpose flour
1 egg and 1 egg white	¼ cup milk
½ tsp. salt	½ cup chopped walnuts
grated rind of 1 orange	¼ cup orange marmalade
2 tsps. baking powder	

Preheat oven to 375°. Blend butter or oil with sugar in the bowl of an electric mixer. Add the egg, egg white, salt, orange rind and liqueur. Then add flour and milk alternately, the nuts, the marmalade and lastly the baking powder. Butter well two 9-inch cake pans and divide batter equally between the two. Bake for 25-30 minutes. When baked, turn out on a cooling rack and, when cool, put layers together with an orange filling. Place a lace paper doily on top of the cake (smooth side down) and sift on confectioner's sugar generously. Then lift doily carefully. This will leave an attractive pattern on the cake.

Pineapple Chartreuse Pâtisserie

Spirit used:
  Yellow chartreuse

3 eggs	1 tsp. baking powder
1 cup white sugar	1 tbsp. butter
¼ cup yellow chartreuse	½ cup light brown sugar
2 tbsps. water	1 #303 can pineapple slices
1 cup sifted flour	(9 slices)

3 tbsps. ground pistachio nuts

Preheat oven to 350°. Separate the eggs. Place the yolks in a bowl, add white sugar and beat until light. Add 1 tbsp. chartreuse and 2 tbsps. water and continue to beat. Add the flour, the egg whites, which have been stiffly beaten, and the baking powder. Grease a 9" x 9" x 2" square pan with the butter, sprinkle on the light brown sugar and 2 tbsps. of the chartreuse. Drain the pineapple slices and arrange them on bottom of pan. Fill holes of slices with ground pistachio nuts and pour batter over. Bake for 35 minutes. Remove, invert on cooling rack and, when cool, transfer to heat-proof platter. When ready to serve, cut cake into portions and flame separately with the remaining chartreuse. Serves 9.

Poncino Bars à la Caruba

Spirit used:
  Jamaican rum

Accompaniment:
  Poncino

¼ cup butter (½ strip)	1¾ cups flour
¼ cup oil	3 bananas, mashed
1 cup light brown sugar	1 tsp. grated lemon rind*
3 eggs	½ cup chopped walnuts
2 tbsps. instant coffee	2 tsps. baking powder

1 or 2 tsps. rum

Preheat oven to 350°. Cream butter, oil and brown sugar in

a large bowl. Add eggs one at a time. Mix instant coffee with flour and add alternately with the mashed bananas. Add lemon rind and walnuts and lastly the baking powder. Pour mixture in a buttered 10" x 13" x 2" pan and bake for approximately 30 minutes. Cool in pan, cut in bars and ice with glaze made by combining ½ cup confectioner's sugar, 1 tsp. instant coffee, and enough rum to bind (1 or 2 tsps.).

* ½ tsp. commercially prepared grated lemon rind equals 1 tsp. freshly grated.

Poncino is Italian black coffee with a dash of rum and a twist of lemon, served in a 6-oz. stemmed glass.

Porcupine Cake

Spirit used:
  Rum

5 squares unsweetened chocolate	½ lb. butter (1 cup)
1 cup coffee—regular strength	12 ladyfingers
4 egg yolks	½ cup rum
¾ cup granulated sugar	3 tbsps. toasted slivered almonds
½ cup cocoa	

Melt chocolate in top of double boiler. Add ¼ cup coffee, stirring until mixture is smooth. Remove pan from over hot water and add yolks one at a time, beating after each addition. Then add sugar. Put pan back over hot water and stir until thick and smooth. Remove pan and add butter bit by bit.

Line a 1-quart melon mold with waxed paper. Split ladyfingers in half lengthwise. Prepare a dip of ½ cup rum and ½ cup coffee, and moisten the ladyfinger halves by dipping them first on one side and then the other. Starting with a layer of ladyfingers, fill mold with alternate layers of ladyfingers and chocolate mixture. Chill until chocolate cream is set and firm —at least two hours.

To serve: Unmold on a serving dish, frost top and sides with chocolate icing made by stirring together ½ cup cocoa, ¼ cup coffee, ¼ cup softened butter, and approximately 1 to 1½ cups confectioner's sugar. For the porcupine effect, stud the surface of the cake with toasted, slivered, blanched almonds.

A delectable dessert from Austria that will keep 3 or 4 days in the refrigerator.

Rumbas

Spirit used:
  Jamaican rum

¼ cup Jamaican rum	½ cup light brown sugar
1 lb. pitted dates	1 cup all-purpose flour
½ cup glazed cherries	¼ tsp. orange bitters
½ cup chopped nuts	3 egg whites

Preheat oven to 350°. Pour rum into a large mixing bowl. Add the dates and cherries which have been cut in small pieces. Add nuts, sugar and flour and mix so that the fruit is well coated. Add the bitters and stiffly beaten egg whites and mix well. Drop by teaspoonfuls on a lightly greased cookie sheet. Bake for 20-25 minutes. Makes 4 dozen.

The rumbas keep very well. In fact, like certain wines, they improve with age.

Sicilian Cheese Cake

Spirit used:
 Crème de cacao

1 lb. creamed cottage cheese
½ cup granulated sugar
1 tsp. almond extract
½ cup crème de cacao
3 tbsps. chocolate bits
3 tbsps. glazed fruits, chopped
sponge cake

Filling: Mix together cottage cheese, sugar, almond extract and half of the crème de cacao. Add chocolate bits and chopped, glazed fruits.

Prepare the 3-egg sponge cake batter given in recipe for Zuppa Inglese Cake, and bake in an 8-inch spring form. Cool and cut in three layers. Put bottom layer back in the spring form, spread half the filling over it, add another layer and spread rest of filling over it. Cover with the third layer (cut side down). Sprinkle rest of crème de cacao over top and place spring form in refrigerator to mellow.

To serve: Remove from spring form, place on cake plate and sprinkle with confectioner's sugar.

Southern Belle Sponge Roll

Spirit used:
 Bourbon

3 eggs, separated
¾ cup sugar
3 tbsps. bourbon
1 cup all-purpose flour
1 tsp. baking powder
1 cup whipped cream flavored with 1 tbsp. bourbon

Preheat oven to 350°. Beat egg yolks and sugar in mixer for 2 or 3 minutes, add bourbon and beat 1 minute more. Fold in quickly the flour, stiffly beaten egg whites and lastly the baking powder. Place on a greased (with corn oil) 11" x 16" cookie tin (tin has sides) and bake 20 to 25 minutes or until light brown. Remove from oven and cover with a damp towel until cool. When cool, dust top with confectioner's sugar and turn out onto a sheet of waxed paper. Spread the flavored whipped cream on top and roll lengthwise. Place on platter and set in refrigerator until ready to serve. Dust again with confectioner's sugar, if necessary. Makes 10 to 12 slices.

Sponge Roll

Spirit used:
  Any fruit liqueur

3 eggs	1 cup all-purpose flour
3 tbsps. water	1 tsp. baking powder
1 cup sugar	1 cup heavy cream, whipped
2 tbsps. fruit liqueur	

Preheat oven to 350°. Separate eggs. To the yolks add water, sugar, flour and baking powder. Mix well and add stiffly beaten egg whites. Bake in buttered, rectangular 12" x 16" cookie tin for 20-25 minutes until lightly golden. Cover with damp towel and cool. When cool, turn out on waxed paper, dust top with confectioner's sugar to dry. Spread with cream which has been whipped with liqueur and roll. Serves 8 to 10.

A most versatile sponge cake that can also be baked in two 8-inch layer cake pans. The layers can be cooled and frozen for later use.

Strufoli

Spirit used:
  Brandy

2 cups sifted, all-purpose flour
pinch salt
3 eggs
¼ tsp. baking powder
1 tbsp. brandy
½ cup honey

½ cup sugar
¼ tsp. ginger
½ cup ground pistachio nuts
silver balls, colored sprinkles, cinnamon balls, etc.

Combine flour, salt, eggs, baking powder and brandy and mix until smooth. Roll out to ¼ inch thickness and cut into strips approximately 5 inches long and ¾ inch wide. Roll these strips between the hands to form cords and cut each cord into ½-inch pieces. Fry in deep hot fat (375°). While they are frying cook honey, sugar and ginger in a very large skillet until syrupy. Toss the cooked pieces in the syrup until each is coated. Have ready a footed cake dish and as each batch is finished, make a pyramid, starting with a wide base and sprinkling on the ground pistachio nuts, some of the colored balls and sprinkles as you go. Work up to a point, tossing on more and more decorations, until it resembles a decorated Christmas tree. Place on center of table or on coffee table and let your guests break off pieces. Serves 12 to 15.

An elaborate, edible Christmas tree centerpiece.

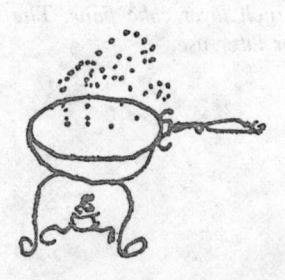

Swedish Apple Cake

Spirit used:
  Cherry brandy

1½ lbs. tart apples (winesaps or star)	1 or 2 tsps. cinnamon
	1 cup bread crumbs
2 tbsps. butter	½ cup cherry brandy
¾ cup dark brown sugar	1 cup heavy cream, whipped
8 tsps. raspberry jam	

Preheat oven to 350°. Peel and cut apples into thin sections (about 16 slices to the apple). In a well buttered baking dish (9" x 6" x 2") arrange a layer of apple slices and sprinkle with brown sugar and cinnamon. Add a layer of bread crumbs, then another layer of apples, sugar and cinnamon until the dish is filled. Pour cherry brandy over top and bake in 350° oven until apples are tender (approximately 40 minutes). Cut into 8 squares. Put 1 tsp. raspberry jam on each portion and surround with whipped cream piped out of pastry bag. Serves 8.

Zuppa Inglese Cake

Spirits used:
  Rum and crème de cacao

1¼ cups sugar	1 tbsp. lemon juice or 1 tsp. dried lemon rind
1⅓ cups flour	
¼ tsp. salt	1 tsp. baking powder
2 cups milk	6 tbsps. Nesselro or glazed fruit
7 eggs	
3 tbsps. water	8 tbsps. rum
	8 tbsps. crème de cacao
1 cup whipped cream and ¼ cup shaved baking chocolate (optional)	

Pastry Cream: Combine ½ cup sugar, ⅓ cup flour, ¼ tsp.

salt in a 1-quart pan. Add 2 cups milk and beat with a wire whisk until well mixed. Gradually add 4 egg yolks (reserving whites for meringue), place pan directly over the fire, and cook until thick. Cool quickly.

Cake: Preheat oven to 350°. Cream egg yolks with ¾ cup sugar until light. Add 3 tbsps. water, 1 tbsp. lemon juice or rind, then 1 cup flour. Beat 3 egg whites until stiff, fold in the yolk mixture, and then add 1 tsp. baking powder. Pour batter into two greased 8-inch cake pans and bake for 25 minutes. Turn out to cool.

To combine: Cut each cake in two layers. Place one layer in the bottom of an 8-inch spring form pan, sprinkle over 2 tbsps. rum and 2 tbsps. crème de cacao, cover with ⅓ of the pastry cream and 2 tbsps. of Nesselro or glazed fruits. Repeat with next two layers and cover with fourth layer. Sprinkle with remaining 2 tbsps. rum and 2 tbsps. crème de cacao. Cover the pan and leave in refrigerator for from 2 days to a week to mellow.

To serve: Preheat oven to 450°. Remove sides of spring form pan and place cake on a heat-proof dish. Beat the 4 remaining egg whites with 2 tbsps. sugar and spread over the cake, being sure that no part is left uncovered. Place in oven for 5 minutes until lightly browned. Bring to the table, flame with 2 tbsps. rum, and serve while still flaming.

For summer serving: Instead of meringue, use 1 cup whipped cream to ice the cake and sprinkle with shaved baking chocolate.

Desserts

Apricot Cream Mold

Spirit used:
 Apricot brandy

1 pkg. gelatin	1 #2 can peeled apricots
¼ cup sugar	½ cup heavy cream
½ tsp. salt	1 egg

¼ cup apricot brandy

Combine gelatin, sugar and salt in a 1-quart saucepan. Add apricot juice, cream and egg yolk and stir until all ingredients are well blended and the gelatin dissolved. Place over low heat and cook until mixture is thick. Do not boil. Place pan in refrigerator or over large bowl of ice cubes. Beat egg white until very stiff and fold into cooled sauce. Slice apricots and add along with brandy. Turn into a 1-quart fancy mold and chill until firm.
To serve: Unmold on a clear glass or milk glass plate and surround with apricot slices.

NOTE: *If apricot slices are not available, halves may be substituted.*

Asti Spumante Mousse with Strawberries

Wine used:
 Asti Spumante*

1 tbsp. gelatin	½ cup sugar
1 cup Asti Spumante	1 cup finely ground almonds
4 eggs, separated	1 cup heavy cream, whipped

1 quart fresh strawberries

Soften gelatin in ¼ cup of Asti Spumante. In a small pot, beat egg yolks and sugar with a wire whisk until they become

light in color (about 5 minutes). Add almonds, softened gelatin and Asti Spumante. Cook and stir until the sauce thickens and then quickly cool the mixture by placing the pan and contents over cubes of ice in a large bowl or in the freezer unit. Add stiffly beaten egg whites and ½ cup of the whipped cream to the cooled sauce and pour into a buttered 1-quart ring mold. Place in refrigerator to set.
To serve: Turn out the mold on a large plate, fill the center with fresh strawberries and remaining ½ cup of whipped cream mixed together. Serves 8.

* *A still wine, such as a Sauternes, Barsac, Semillon or Chardonnay may be substituted for Asti Spumante.*

Bananas al Cordial

Wine and spirit used:
  Ruby port and rum or brandy

8 green-tipped bananas
½ cup light brown sugar
¼ tsp. cinnamon
¼ tsp. nutmeg
1 cup macaroons, crushed
1 cup ruby port
¼ cup rum or brandy

Preheat oven to 400°. Peel bananas, cut in half lengthwise, then crosswise, so that each one is quartered. Butter a 1-quart casserole, put in a layer of bananas and dust with brown sugar, cinnamon, nutmeg and finely crushed macaroons.
Repeat layers until casserole is full. Pour over 1 cup ruby port and any left-over macaroons. Bake for approximately 30 minutes. Flame at the table with rum or brandy.

A very popular Madrid dessert.

Bananas Chartreuse

Spirit used:
 Yellow chartreuse

4 green-tipped bananas   1 tbsp. sugar
1 tbsp. butter   pinch dry ginger
          ¼ cup yellow chartreuse

Peel bananas and cut in half lengthwise, then crosswise. Melt butter in top pan of chafing dish and add banana quarters. Sauté until lightly brown, turn and sauté one minute longer. Sprinkle with sugar and ginger. Pour yellow chartreuse over, flame and serve immediately. Serves 6 to 8.

A simple and delightful dessert to be prepared at the table.

Banana Soufflé Flambé

Spirit used:
 Brandy, rum or banana liqueur

6 ripe bananas   3 tbsps. ground almonds
1 orange   4 egg whites
½ cup granulated sugar   pinch of salt
          3 tbsps. brandy, rum or banana liqueur

Preheat oven to 375°. Mash bananas and mix with grated rind and juice of orange (approximately ½ cup juice and 1 tbsp. rind), sugar and almonds. Beat egg whites until very stiff, add salt and blend with banana-orange mixture. Bake in buttered 1-quart soufflé dish for 30 minutes or until puffed and golden. Serve at once and flame at the table with brandy, rum or banana liqueur. Serves 6 to 8.

Bread Pudding Supreme

Spirit used:
  Fruit liqueur*

2 tbsps. butter	2 cups dry bread cubes
3 cups milk	¼ cup fruit liqueur*
4 eggs	jam*
¼ cup sugar	

Preheat oven to 375°. Heat butter and milk together until lukewarm. In large bowl beat 2 whole eggs, 2 egg yolks and ¼ cup sugar until light in color (5 minutes). Pour in lukewarm milk mixture and stir. Add bread cubes and liqueur and mix thoroughly. Bake in a buttered 1-quart casserole for 30 minutes. Remove from the oven and spread the top with jam. Beat remaining 2 egg whites until stiff, spread over pudding and return to oven until meringue is slightly brown (5 minutes). Serves 6-8.

Use a liqueur and a jam of the same flavor—apricot liqueur and apricot jam; orange liqueur and orange jam, and so forth.

Cherry Sauce

Spirit used:
  Cherry brandy

1 cup fresh or canned red cherries	½ cup sugar syrup
	¼ cup cherry brandy

Combine ingredients and pour over ice cream, cake or pudding.

Variations on the theme: Combine any fruit brandy with sugar syrup and the fruit from which the brandy is made.

NOTE: *Sugar syrup (or simple syrup) is made by boiling gently 1 cup water and 1 cup granulated sugar together for 5 minutes. Can be stored in a pint jar for use in various drinks and sauces.*

Chocolate-Orange Mousse

Spirit used:
  Orange liqueur

1 pkg. chocolate bits (6 oz.)	1 tbsp. gelatin
3 tbsps. water	¼ cup orange juice
3 eggs	1 cup heavy cream, whipped
½ cup sugar	2 tbsps. orange liqueur

Melt chocolate bits in water over low heat. Beat eggs and sugar together and add chocolate-water mixture. Soften gelatin in orange juice and place bowl in 2 inches of hot water to liquefy. Add liqueur to whipped cream and then add the gelatin mixture to the egg and chocolate mixture. Fold in whipped cream mixture. Blend all together and pour into a lightly oiled soufflé dish. Place in refrigerator until set. Serves 6 to 8.

Oranges are to chocolate as nectar is to ambrosia.

Chocolate-Rum Mousse

Spirit used:
  Rum or brandy

1 pkg. chocolate chips	1 tbsp. rum or brandy
3 tbsps. water	5 eggs

For this French dessert melt chocolate chips in water over a low fire. When melted, remove from fire and stir in rum. Separate eggs and beat chocolate mixture into the yolks. Beat whites separately and fold in. Pour into 4-ounce custard cups or pots and chill in refrigerator for at least 4 hours before serving. (Will keep for a week in refrigerator.) Serves 8.

Eggnog Chiffon Pie

Spirits used:
Brandy and rum

1 tbsp. gelatin	pinch salt
2 tbsps. cold water	½ tsp. nutmeg
⅔ cup milk	3 tbsps. brandy
3 eggs, separated	2 tbsps. rum
½ cup sugar	1 tsp. vanilla

1 cup heavy cream, whipped
1 baked, deep, 8″ fruit pie shell

Soften gelatin in cold water. Scald milk in the top of a double boiler, directly over the fire. Add egg yolks, half the sugar, the salt, nutmeg and softened gelatin. Cook and stir over hot water until gelatin is dissolved and the custard is thick. Add brandy, rum and vanilla and stir well.

Remove pan from hot water and chill. Beat the egg whites with remaining sugar until stiff and add to the milk mixture when cooled. Fold in whipped cream, reserving some for decoration, and pour into baked pie shell. Decorate top with remaining whipped cream and sprinkle with freshly grated nutmeg. Serves 8.

Fig Soufflé

Spirit used:
Brandy

1 #2½ can of figs	pinch salt
2 tbsps. sugar	½ tsp. lemon juice
4 tbsps. brandy	3 tbsps. shredded almonds
4 egg whites	½ cup whipped cream

Preheat oven to 375°. Put figs through coarse strainer and heat in pan with sugar and 3 tbsps. of the brandy over a low flame until warm. Remove from flame. Beat egg whites very stiff, add salt and lemon juice and fold into the fig mixture. Sprinkle the bottom of a buttered 1-quart soufflé dish with the almonds and pour fig mixture over. Bake for 30 minutes until top is puffed and golden. Serve at once with a side dish of whipped cream flavored with 1 tbsp. brandy. Serves 6.

Fruit Timbale

Spirit used:
  Rum

½ cup unwashed rice
4 egg yolks
½ cup sugar
¾ cup milk
1 tsp. vanilla

¾ cup Nesselro*
¼ cup rum
1 cup heavy cream, whipped
1 tbsp. gelatin
1 2-oz. jar glazed cherries

Boil rice in 5-quart pot for 13 minutes. Drain in colander and rinse with cold water. Place rice in colander over 2 inches of water in pot and steam for 15 minutes.

Sauce: In top of double boiler put egg yolks, sugar, milk and vanilla and cook over hot water until sauce is smooth and thick. Add Nesselro, rum and most of the whipped cream, reserving some for decoration. Lastly add gelatin which has been softened in 2 tbsps. water and steamed rice. Pour into fancy 1-quart mold and chill until ready to serve. Turn out on a platter and decorate top with glazed cherries and rest of whipped cream.

Nesselro is a trade name for fruits in rum.

Grand Marnier Mousse

Spirits used:
Grand Marnier and brandy

1 tbsp. gelatin	¼ cup brandy
¼ cup cold milk	¼ cup Grand Marnier
3 eggs	1 cup heavy cream, whipped
3 tbsps. sugar	12 ladyfingers

shredded rind of one orange

Soften gelatin in milk and dissolve over hot water. Separate eggs and beat yolks with sugar until light in color. Add brandy, then Grand Marnier. Mix and add stiffly beaten egg whites and whipped cream and lastly the softened gelatin. Blend. Line a deep (1 quart) serving dish with the ladyfingers which have been split in half lengthwise. Pour in the mixture and sprinkle top with shredded orange rind. Chill at least 4 hours in refrigerator before serving and serve directly from dish. Serves 6 to 8.

Very delicate—very French.

Grand Marnier Soufflé

Spirit used:
Grand Marnier

3 tbsps. butter	¼ cup granulated sugar
3 tbsps. flour	pinch salt
1 cup light cream	½ cup Grand Marnier
4 eggs, separated	3 ladyfingers

Preheat oven to 375°. Melt butter in a 1-quart pan, remove from fire and stir in flour. Add cream and cook while stirring until thickened. Beat egg yolks, salt and sugar together and add to the sauce mixture. Add ¼ cup Grand Marnier and fold in stiffly beaten egg whites.

Cut ladyfingers in half lengthwise and moisten with ¼ cup Grand Marnier. Butter a 1-quart soufflé dish, pour in half the mixture, arrange the moistened ladyfinger halves on top and cover with rest of mixture. Bake for 30 minutes. Serve hot. Serves 6.

Close your eyes and you're dining at Lucien's in Paris.

Hot Chocolate Soufflé

Spirit used:
  Brandy

3 tbsps. butter	½ tsp. vanilla
3 tbsps. flour	pinch salt
1 cup milk	½ tsp. orange bitters
¼ cup sugar	2 tbsps. brandy
2 squares unsweetened chocolate	4 eggs, separated
	whipped cream

Preheat oven to 375°. Melt butter in a 1-quart pan and stir in flour away from fire. Add milk and sugar. Return to a low heat and stir until sauce thickens. Melt chocolate in small bowl over hot water, add to sauce, then add vanilla, salt, bitters, 1 tbsp. brandy and egg yolks. Beat egg whites stiff and fold into chocolate mixture. Lightly butter a 1-quart soufflé dish. Make a collar of buttered wax paper by tying with a string a double thickness of the paper in a band around the outside of the soufflé dish. Pour in soufflé and bake for 30 minutes. Serve with whipped cream flavored with 1 tbsp. brandy. Serves 6 to 8.

Kestane Sekeri (Turkish Chestnut Dessert)

Spirit used:
  Rum

1 cup puréed chestnuts*   3 tbsps. sugar
pinch salt   4 eggs, separated
2 tbsps. heavy cream   1 tsp. vanilla
                3 tbsps. rum

Preheat oven to 350°. Using fork, mix in a bowl the puréed chestnuts, salt, cream, sugar and egg yolks. Fold in the stiffly beaten egg whites and then the vanilla and rum. Pour into a greased 1-quart baking dish and bake for 30 minutes or until lightly brown on top. May be served hot or cold with a side dish of rum-flavored whipped cream. Serves 8.

* Puréed, cooked chestnuts are sold in one- and two-pound cans.

Mocha Mousse

Spirit used:
  Coffee liqueur

1 pkg. chocolate bits   5 egg yolks
¼ cup coffee liqueur   5 egg whites

Melt chocolate bits in 1-quart pan over low heat until dissolved. Remove from fire, stir in coffee liqueur, add egg yolks and beat until light. Cool. Beat egg whites until stiff and fold chocolate mixture into them. Pour into custard cups or mugs. Place in refrigerator for three hours or until set. Serves 8.

Orange Mousse

Spirit used:
  Orange liqueur

3 whole eggs
2 egg yolks
dash orange bitters
3 tbsps. sugar
grated rind of 1 large navel orange
1 tbsp. gelatin
¼ cup orange juice
¼ cup whipped cream
¼ cup orange liqueur
orange sections
2 tbsps. currant jelly

Put eggs, egg yolks, bitters and sugar in large bowl and beat with rotary beater until mixture is very thick. Add grated orange rind and keep beating until the rind is incorporated. Soften gelatin in orange juice and place dish in 1 inch of hot water until gelatin is completely liquefied. Combine with egg mixture. Fold in whipped cream and add orange liqueur. Blend all ingredients well and pour into 1-quart mold or fancy dish. Chill in refrigerator until set.
To serve: Unmold on plate, garnish with peeled orange sections, and pour over currant jelly, which has been melted in small pan directly over fire. Serves 8.

This delightful dish may be prepared in individual molds, if preferred.

Peach Bowl

Wine and spirit used:
  Brandy and champagne

1 fresh peach
1 oz. brandy
6 ozs. champagne

This is a classic dessert, but may be served as an appetizer.

In a champagne glass or sherbet glass place a perfect fresh peach, peeled. Prick the peach with the tines of a fork, pour brandy over it and fill the glass with champagne. One portion.

Just right for visiting royalty.

Pineapple Soufflé

Spirit used:
  Brandy

3 tbsps. butter
3 tbsps. flour
1 #303 can of crushed pineapple
¼ cup brandy
¼ cup sugar
4 eggs, separated
1 tbsp. lemon juice
½ cup whipped cream (optional)

Preheat oven to 375°. Melt butter in a 1-quart pan, remove from heat and add flour, stirring to incorporate it. Drain pineapple, add pineapple juice, brandy, sugar and egg yolks to butter and flour mixture. Mix well, put back on fire, and stir until the mixture thickens. Add pineapple, stiffly beaten egg whites and lemon juice. Stir a minute to blend and pour into a 1-quart buttered soufflé dish. Bake in a 375° oven for 30 minutes. Serve with whipped cream or flame with 2 tbsps. brandy. Serves 6.

Pumpkin Rum Soufflé

Spirit used:
  Rum

- 2 tbsps. butter
- 3 tbsps. flour
- ¾ cup milk
- 4 eggs, separated
- 1½ cups strained cooked pumpkin
- ½ cup dark brown sugar
- 3 tbsps. orange juice
- ¼ tsp. salt
- ¼ cup light or dark rum
- ½ tsp. nutmeg
- ¼ tsp. cinnamon
- 1 tsp. dry ginger

Melt butter in 2-quart saucepan, remove from fire and add flour. Stir in milk and egg yolks. Cook while stirring until thick. Remove from fire and add pumpkin, sugar, orange juice, salt, rum, and spices. When all ingredients are well blended, put pan back on the fire for a minute to reheat, then away from the heat again to add the stiffly beaten egg whites. Bake in a 1-quart soufflé dish for 30 minutes at 375°. Serve immediately. Serves 6 to 8.

Queen's Pudding (Chocolate Mint Bread Pudding)

Spirit used:
  Crème de Menthe—preferably white

- 3 cups milk
- 2 squares bitter chocolate
- 3 eggs
- ½ cup sugar
- 8 slices stale bread
- 3 tbsps. crème de menthe—preferably white
- 2 tbsps. crushed peppermint candy

Preheat oven to 375°. Heat chocolate in milk until melted. Pour into large bowl and add egg yolks which have been beaten with sugar. Cut the bread in small cubes and add.

Then add crème de menthe. Let soak for approximately 10 minutes or until bread absorbs the liquid. Grease a 1-quart soufflé dish, pour in the mixture and bake for 30-35 minutes. Remove from oven and cover with the stiffly beaten white of one egg flavored with the peppermint candy. Return to the oven for 5 minutes or until meringue is browned. Serve hot. Serves 6-8.

A peerless pudding from England.

Sherry Pie

Wine used:
  Amontillado sherry

Pie Crust:
Mix 1½ cups crushed, chocolate ice box cookies (*plain chocolate thins*) with ¼ cup melted butter and line a 9" pie plate.

Filling:
3 eggs, separated
1 cup milk
½ cup sugar
1 tbsp. gelatin
¼ tsp. salt
½ cup sherry
1 cup whipped cream
¼ cup freshly ground pecans or walnuts

Cook egg yolks, ¾ cup milk and sugar in top of double boiler for 10 minutes or until custard thickens. Add gelatin which has been softened in ¼ cup milk, and salt. Remove from fire and add sherry, stiffly beaten egg whites and whipped cream. Pour into prepared pie crust and put in refrigerator overnight to mellow. Before serving, sprinkle with freshly ground nutmeats. Serves 8.

Strawberry Cream

Spirit used:
Kirsch

4 eggs, separated	¼ cup kirsch
¼ cup sugar	2 cups heavy cream
1 cup milk	2 quarts fresh strawberries

In a small pan beat the yolks of the eggs until light and combine with sugar and milk. Stir over low heat until thickened, add kirsch, and cool. Whip cream and add stiffly beaten egg whites. Fold into custard and chill. Wash, hull and dry strawberries. Serve on chilled plate with custard poured over them. Serves 10-12.

Strawberries Romanoff

Spirit used:
Orange liqueur

1 quart fresh or frozen strawberries	1 cup heavy cream
¼ cup orange liqueur	6 almond macaroons, crushed

Wash and dry fresh strawberries (or defrost frozen ones). Put in a bowl, add orange liqueur and let steep for half an hour. Whip cream until very stiff and add berries (reserving prettiest ones for decorating), juice and liqueur from bowl, and half the crushed macaroons. Stir quickly to incorporate and pour into serving bowl. Place bowl over ice, sprinkle the remaining crushed macaroons over the top and make a border of remaining berries. Or, if you prefer, pour into champagne glasses, sprinkle with crushed macaroons and decorate each with a single berry.

This delectable dessert may be made ahead of time and kept in the refrigerator.

Syllabub

Spirit used:
  Sherry, port or Madeira

¾ cup granulated sugar
juice of 1 lemon (3 tbsps.)
½ cup sherry, port or
  Madeira

2 cups heavy cream, whipped
pinch cinnamon
pinch nutmeg
left-over cake

In a 3-quart bowl, mix the sugar with lemon juice. Add the wine gradually and when the sugar is dissolved, fold in the whipped cream, to which the spices have been added, folding as slowly as possible. As you fold, the cream will get thicker. *To serve:* Place a round of left-over cake in the bottom of each of 12 sherbet glasses, cover with whipped cream mixture and serve very cold. Serves 12.

A traditional English dessert.

Zabaglione

Wine used:
  Marsala, Muscatel or sherry

6 egg yolks   ½ cup granulated sugar
      ¾ cup Marsala, Muscatel or sherry

Traditionally, Marsala is used in Italy to prepare this wine custard, but it is equally delicious if other wines are used. Put egg yolks and sugar in top pan of chafing dish or double boiler and beat with a wire whisk until the mixture becomes slightly lighter in color and the sugar is dissolved. Slowly beat in the wine and continue to beat until the mixture thickens. Remove from fire and serve immediately in small ramekins with ladyfingers or in mugs.

In Italy Zabaglione is served to usher in the New Year.

Zabaglione Sauce

Wine used:
Marsala, Aleatico, sherry or Muscatel

1 whole egg
1 egg yolk
2 tbsps. sugar

¼ cup Marsala, Aleatico, sherry, or Muscatel

Cook the egg, egg yolk, sugar and wine in top of double boiler, beating constantly with a wire whisk until it is fluffy and thick. (Be careful not to cook too long, as it must pour.) Serve over soufflé, cake or pudding.

INDEX

Apricot
  Bars, 141
  Cream Mold, 159
Aspic
  Beef and Vegetable, 65
  Pâté de Foie Gras en, 68
  Shrimp, 70
Asti Spumante Mousse with Strawberries, 159
Austrian Pot Roast with Horseradish, 105
Avocado, Swedish, 139

Baba au Rhum, New Orleans Style, 142
Babka, 143
Baked German Pancakes, 65
Baked Shrimp Casserole, 73
Baked Vegetables Brazilian, 121
Baked Western Steak, 105
Banana Bread, 127
Banana Soufflé Flambé, 161
Bananas al Cordial, 160
Bananas Chartreuse, 161
Barbecue Sauce, 131
Barbecued Potted Beef, 106
Béarnaise Sauce, 131

Béchamel Sauce (White Sauce), 132
Beef
  and Beer Stew, 107
  and Vegetable Aspic, 65
  Austrian Pot Roast with Horseradish, 105
  Baked Western Steak, 105
  Barbecued Potted Beef, 106
  Boeuf à la Bourguignonne, 108
  Braciola (Rolled Beef with Red Wine), 109
  Braised with Red Wine, 110
  California Pepper Steak, 111
  Chili con Carne y Frijoles, 112
  Sauerbraten, 117
  Steak Diane, 118
  Sukiyaki, 118
Beer Bread, 127
Benlose Fugle (Danish Veal Rolls), 107
Bigarade Sauce for Roast Duck and Game Birds, 132

Boeuf à la Bourguignonne, 108
Bordelaise Sauce for Steak or Roasts, 133
Bouillabaisse à la Caen (simplified), 55
Braciola (Rolled Beef with Red Wine), 109
Braised Beef with Red Wine, 110
Braised Leg of Lamb Bordeaux, 110
Bread
 Banana, 127
 Beer, 127
 Christmas Panetone, 128
 Jamaican Date and Nut, 129
Bread Pudding Supreme, 162
Burgundy Onions, 121

Cabbage, Red, with Wine, 124
Cake
 German Beer Cake, 147
 Happy Apple, 149
 Orange Tipple, 150
 Porcupine, 152
 Swedish Apple, 157
California Pepper Steak, 111
Canard Bigarade (Duckling with Orange), 91
Canard Maison (Duckling with Cherries), 92
Capon au Champagne, 93
Carrots, Glazed Supreme, 123
Casserole
 Baked Shrimp, 73
 Poulet en Casserole, 102
Cauliflower Loaf, 122
Caviar and Egg Mousse, 47
Chartreuse Pancakes, 66
Cherry Sauce, 162
Chicken
 and Gin on the Spit, 96
 Cacciatora Piemontese, 94
 Capon au Champagne, 93
 Cornish Hen Plymouth, 98
 Coq au Vin, 97
 Crème de Volaille, 100
 Divan, 95
 Glazed Breasts of, 101
 Paella, 88
 Poulet en Casserole, 102
 Puerto Rican, 103
 with Almonds, 94
 with Olives, 97
Chili con Carne y Frijoles, 112
Chinese Egg Rolls, 48
Christmas Panetone, 128
Chocolate
 Hot Soufflé, 167
 Mint Bread Pudding (Queen's Pudding), 171
 -Orange Mousse, 163
 Rum Chips, 144
 -Rum Mousse, 163
Coffee Bavarian Cream Cake, 143

INDEX

Cookies
  Apricot Bars, 141
  Chocolate Rum Chips, 144
  Fudge Rounds, 146
  Gin and Butter Wafers, 148
  Poncino Bars à la Caruba, 151
Coq au Vin, 97
Cornish Hen Plymouth, 98
Côtellette de Veau, 112
Crab, Mousseline de Crabe, 86
Crabmeat and Bacon Balls, 49
Cream of Cucumber Soup, 56
Cream of Watercress Soup, 57
Crème de Volaille, 82
Crowning Glory (Cream Puff Ring), 145
Cumberland Sauce for Game, 133

Desserts
  Apricot Cream Mold, 159
  Asti Spumante Mousse with Strawberries, 159
  Baba au Rhum, New Orleans Style, 142
  Babka, 143
  Bananas al Cordial, 160
  Bananas Chartreuse, 161
  Banana Soufflé Flambé, 161
  Bread Pudding Supreme, 162
  Coffee Bavarian Cream Cake, 143
  Crowning Glory (Cream Puff Ring), 145
  Fruit Timbale, 165
  Gingerbread, 149
  Kestane Sekeri, 168
  Peach Bowl, 169
  Pineapple Chartreuse Pâtisserie, 151
  Queen's Pudding, 171
  Rumbas, 153
  Sicilian Cheese Cake, 154
  Southern Belle Sponge Roll, 154
  Sponge Roll, 155
  Strawberries Romanoff, 173
  Strawberry Cream, 173
  Strufoli, 131
  Syllabub, 174
  Zabaglione, 174
  Zuppa Inglese Cake, 157
Dijon, Sauce for Steaks, 135
Duck
  Baroque, 67
  Canard Bigarade (Duckling with Orange), 91
  Canard Maison (Duckling with Cherries), 92
  Duckling Marengo, 99
  Provençale, 101
Duchesse Potatoes, 122

Eggnog
  Chiffon Pie, 164
Eggs
  Chinese Egg Rolls, 48
  Scotch Omelet, 69

Fig Soufflé, 164
Filet of Sole
  Cordova, 74
  Dugleré, 75
  Joinville, 76
  Marguery, 77
  Maroca, 78
  Walewska, 79
Filling, French Apricot, for Sponge Roll, 146
Fish
  Filet of Sole Cordova, 74
  Filet of Sole Dugleré, 75
  Filet of Sole Joinville, 76
  Filet of Sole Marguery, 77
  Filet of Sole Maroca, 78
  Filet of Sole Walewska, 79
  Poached in Beer, 80
Flaky Pie Crust, 137
Fondue Helvetia, 50
French Apricot Filling for Sponge Roll, 146
French Onion Soup, 57
Fruit
  Stuffing for Fowl, 137
Fruit Timbale, 165
Fudge Rounds, 146

Gazpacho, 58
Glazed Chicken Breasts, 101
Glazed Carrots Supreme, 123
German Beer Cake, 147
Gin and Butter Wafers, 148
Gingerbread, 149
Grand Marnier Mousse, 166
Grand Marnier Soufflé, 166

Ham and Bourbon Balls, 49
Happy Apple Cake, 149
Hawaiian Salad Dressing, 138
Helvetia Fondue, 50
Hollandaise Sauce, 134
Honey-Orange Dressing for Fruit Salad, 138
Hot Chocolate Soufflé, 167

Italian Holiday Soup with Meatballs, 59

Jamaican Date and Nut Bread, 129
Jellied Cucumber Salad, 139

Kestane Sekeri (Turkish Chestnut Dessert), 168

Lamb,
  Braised Leg, Bordeaux, 110
  Steaks à la Mode, 113

INDEX

Lobster
  à la Newburg, 83
  and Shrimp Bahas, 84
  Cordon Bleu, 81
  Flambé, 82
  in Shells, 83
  Norwegian Bisque of, 62
  Rumaki, 51
  Scottish, 70
  Supreme, 68

Minestrone, Tuscan Style, 60
Minestra di Pasta e Fagioli (Bean Soup with Vegetables), 59
Mocha Mousse, 168
Mornay Sauce, 134
Mousse
  Asti Spumante with Strawberries, 159
  Caviar and Egg, 47
  Chocolate-Orange, 163
  Chocolate-Rum, 163
  Grand Marnier, 166
  Mocha, 168
  Orange, 169
Mousseline de Crabe, 86
Mushroom Soup, 61

Norwegian Lobster Bisque, 62
Norwegian Strawberry Soup, 62

Omelet, Scotch, 69
Onions
  Aleatico, 123
  Burgundy, 121
Orange Mousse, 169
Orange Tipple Cake, 150
Ossobuco Piemontese, 114
Oysters
  Madeira, 86
  Royale, 87

Paella, 88
Pancakes
  Baked German, 65
  Chartreuse, 66
Party Pinwheels, 52
Pâté de Foie Gras en Aspic, 68
Paupiettes de Veau aux Truffes (Rolled Veal with Truffles), 115
Peach Bowl, 169
Pie
  Crust, Flaky, 137
  Eggnog Chiffon, 164
  Sherry, 172
Pineapple
  Chartreuse Pâtisserie, 151
  Soufflé, 170
Poncino Bars à la Caruba, 151
Porcupine Cake, 152
Potatoes, Duchesse, 122
Poulet en Casserole, 102
Puerto Rican Chicken, 103
Pumpkin Rum Soufflé, 171

Queen's Pudding (Chocolate Mint Bread Pudding), 171

Red Cabbage with Wine, 124
Roquefort and Whiskey Spread, 52
Rumbas, 153

Saddle of Venison with Bourbon, 116
Salad, Jellied Cucumber, 139
Salad Dressing, Hawaiian, 138
Salad Dressing, Honey-Orange, for Fruit Salad, 138
Saltimbocca, 116
Sauce
  Barbecue, 131
  Béarnaise, 131
  Béchamel (White Sauce), 132
  Bigarade, for Roast Duck and Game Birds, 132
  Bordelaise, for Steak or Roasts, 133
  Cherry, 162
  Cumberland for Game, 133
  Dijon for Steaks, 135
  Hollandaise, 134
  Mornay, 134
  Spaghetti, alla Piemontese, 136

Zabaglione, 175
Sauerbraten, 117
Scotch Omelet, 69
Scottish Lobster, 70
Sherry Pie, 172
Shrimp
  and Lobster Bahas, 84
  Aspic, 70
  Baked Casserole of, 73
  in Sherry, 53
  Marinière, 89
  Tempura, 90
Sicilian Cheese Cake, 154
Soufflé
  Banana Flambé, 161
  Fig, 164
  Grand Marnier, 166
  Hot Chocolate, 167
  Pineapple, 170
  Pumpkin Rum, 171
Soups
  Bouillabaisse à la Caen, (simplified), 55
  Cream of Cucumber, 56
  Cream of Watercress, 57
  French Onion, 57
  Gazpacho, 58
  Italian Holiday with Meatballs, 59
  Minestra di Pasta e Fagioli (Bean Soup with Vegetables), 59
  Minestrone–Tuscan Style, 60
  Mushroom, 61
  Norwegian Lobster Bisque, 62

INDEX

Soups *(cont'd)*
   Norwegian Strawberry, 62
Southern Belle Sponge Roll, 154
Spaghetti Sauce alla Piemontese, 136
Sponge Roll, 155
Steak Diane, 118
Stew, Beef and Beer, 107
Strawberries Romanoff, 173
Strawberry Cream, 173
Strufoli, 156
Stuffing, Fruit for Fowl, 137
Sukiyaki, 118
Swedish Apple Cake, 157
Swedish Avocado, 139
Sweet Potato Puffs, 125
Sweetbreads d'Anjou, 119
Syllabub, 174

Tongue à la Duchess of Windsor, 71
Truffles, Paupiettes de Veau aux Truffes, (Rolled Veal with Truffles), 115
Turkish Chestnut Dessert (Kestane Sekeri), 168

Veal
   Côtelette de Veau, 112
   Ossobuco Piemontese, 114
   Paupiettes de Veau aux Truffes (Rolled Veal with Truffles), 115
   Rolls, Danish (Benlose Fugle), 107
   Saltimbocca, 116
   Scallopini alla Romano, 120
Venison, Saddle of, with Bourbon, 116

Wild Rice, 140
Zabaglione, 174
Zabaglione Sauce, 175
Zuppa Inglese Cake, 157